REBUILDING LOVE: A JOURNEY OF FORGIVENESS AND GROWTH

REBUILDING LOVE: A JOURNEY OF FORGIVENESS AND GROWTH

A Journey of Forgiveness and Growth

DAVID OLUBIYI

Dabim Support Services Inc.

Contents

Dedication ix
Foreword xi
Introduction xiii

One
The Beginning — 1

Two
The First Sign — 5

Three
The Second Sign — 8

Four
The Third Sign — 12

Five
The Breaking Point — 16

Six
The Decision — 19

Seven
The Apology — 22

Eight
The First Step — 26

Nine
The Therapy   29

Ten
The Progress   34

Eleven
The Setback   37

Twelve
The Support System   40

Thirteen
The Doubts   42

Fourteen
The Reflection   45

Fifteen
The Changes   48

Sixteen
The Realization   50

Seventeen
The Reconciliation   52

Eighteen
The Renewed commitment   55

Nineteen
The Relapse   58

Twenty
The Reminder   61

Twenty-One
The Patience   63

Twenty-Two
The Trust   65

Twenty-Three
The Appreciation …… 69

Twenty-Four
The Forgiveness …… 72

Twenty-Five
The Self-Care …… 74

Twenty-Six
The Intimacy …… 77

Twenty-Seven
The Communication …… 80

Twenty-Eight
The Growth …… 83

Twenty-Nine
The Milestones …… 85

Thirty
The Reflections …… 88

Thirty-One
The Gratitude …… 90

Thirty-Two
The Goals …… 92

Thirty-Three
The Support …… 95

Thirty-Four
The Challenges …… 97

Thirty-Five
The Reflection …… 99

Thirty-Six
The Renewed Vows …… 101

Thirty-Seven
The Trust Issues   103

Thirty-Eight
The Openness   105

Thirty-Nine
The Anniversary   108

Forty
The Reflection   111

Forty-One
The Empathy   113

Forty-Two
The Growth Mindset   116

Forty-Three
The Resilience   119

Forty-Four
The Gratefulness   121

Forty-Five
The Forever After   123

Conclusion   125
Acknowledgement   127

DEDICATION

To my beloved wife and precious children,

This book would not have been possible without your unwavering love, support, and encouragement. You have been my constant source of inspiration and motivation, always pushing me to pursue my dreams and never give up on my passions.

My wife, you are the love of my life, my partner in everything. Your love and support have been the backbone of our family. Your patience, understanding, and belief in me have been the driving force behind this book. I dedicate this book to you, my dear wife, as a token of my love and appreciation for all that you do for our family.

My children, you are my pride and joy. Your innocent laughter, boundless energy, and unwavering faith in me make every day brighter. I dedicate this book to you, my dear children, as a testament to the love and joy you bring into my life.

May this book serve as a reminder of the love and gratitude I have for my family, and may it inspire others to cherish their loved ones just as much.

Copyright © 2023 by David Olubiyi

All rights reserved. No part of this book may be reproduced in any manner whatsoever without written permission except in the case of brief quotations embodied in critical articles and reviews.

First Printing, 2023

Foreword

Love is a beautiful thing, but it is not always easy. When a relationship faces challenges, it can be difficult to know how to move forward. David Olubiyi's book, "Rebuilding Love," provides a roadmap for couples who want to strengthen their relationship and rebuild trust.

The story of Evelyn and Adam is not just a love story, but a story of resilience, growth, and forgiveness. It shows that even when things seem impossible, there is always a way to rebuild and move forward.

In this book, Olubiyi shares the story of Evelyn and Adam, a couple whose marriage is on the brink of collapse after a series of trust issues. Through their journey, we see the power of forgiveness, communication, and commitment in rebuilding a strong and healthy relationship.

Olubiyi's writing is clear, concise, and relatable. He provides practical advice and exercises for couples to work through their issues together. As a therapist, Olubiyi has seen firsthand the damage that can be done to a relationship when trust is broken, but he has also seen the transformative power of love and commitment in repairing that damage.

"Rebuilding Love" is not just for couples who are struggling. It is a valuable resource for anyone who wants to deepen their understanding of what it takes to build and maintain a healthy relationship. Whether you are in a committed relationship or simply looking for tools to strengthen your connections with others, this book will provide you with valuable insights and strategies.

I am honored to introduce this book to you and I hope that it will inspire and guide you in your own journey of love and commitment.

Introduction

Love is one of the most complex emotions humans experience. It can bring immense joy and fulfillment, but it can also be the source of pain and heartbreak. Relationships can be fragile and require constant effort to maintain. But what happens when that effort falls short and a relationship breaks down?

In this book, "Rebuilding Love", we follow the journey of Evelyn and Adam as they navigate the challenges of a broken marriage and work to rebuild their love. Their story is a testament to the resilience and power of love when two committed individuals are willing to fight for it.

Through their ups and downs, we witness the importance of communication, empathy, forgiveness, and trust. We see the power of vulnerability and how it can strengthen relationships. And we learn the value of perseverance and the willingness to embrace growth and change.

This book is not just a story of two people, but a guidebook for anyone looking to rebuild a broken relationship. Whether you are dealing with infidelity, communication issues, or other relationship challenges, the lessons in this book can be applied to your own life.

Join Evelyn and Adam on their journey and discover the transformative power of rebuilding love.

One

The Beginning

Evelyn met the love of her life, Adam, in college. They got married right after graduation, and she thought that they would live happily ever after. But as time went on, Evelyn started to notice that their relationship wasn't as perfect as she thought it was.

* * *

Evelyn was a college student who had always believed in the power of love. She was a romantic at heart and dreamed of finding her happily ever after. When she met Adam, she knew that he was the one for her.

Adam was everything she wanted in a partner. He was kind, funny, and intelligent. They shared the same interests and had similar goals in life. It wasn't long before they started dating, and soon after, they fell deeply in love.

As they navigated through their college years, they shared countless conversations that helped them build a strong bond and support system.

"Do you ever feel like you're not good enough?" she asked him one night as they sat on the roof of their dorm, looking out at the city skyline.

"All the time," he replied honestly. "But then I remind myself that I'm here for a reason, and that I'm capable of achieving my goals."

"I needed to hear that," she said, smiling at him. "You always know just what to say."

Another time, as they explored a new part of the city, she turned to him and said, "I can't imagine going through college without you. You make everything so much better."

"I feel the same way," he replied. "I don't think I could have made it this far without you by my side."

Through the ups and downs of college life, they leaned on each other for support and guidance. They knew that no matter what challenges they faced, they could always count on each other to be there.

After graduation, Adam proposed to Evelyn, He nervously got down on one knee and pulled out a small velvet box from his pocket. "Evelyn, my love, will you do me the honor of becoming my wife?" he asked, holding the box out to her.

Evelyn's eyes widened in surprise and joy as she looked down at the box. "Oh my goodness, Adam!" she exclaimed, feeling her heart race. "Yes! Yes, I will marry you!"

A few months later, as they stood at the altar surrounded by their loved ones, Adam took Evelyn's hand in his and whispered, "I can't believe I'm marrying my best friend. You make me so happy, Evelyn."

Evelyn smiled back at him, her eyes shining with love. "You make me happy too, Adam. I can't wait to spend the rest of my life with you."

Evelyn thought that their marriage would be perfect, just like their college years. She believed that they were meant to be together, and nothing could ever come between them.

But as time passed, Evelyn began to notice that things were not the same between her and Adam. He seemed distant, and they started having more arguments than usual. Concerned about their relationship, Evelyn tried talking to him about it.

Evelyn: "Adam, I've been noticing that you seem a bit distant lately. Is everything okay?"

Adam: "Yeah, everything's fine. Don't worry about it."

Evelyn: "But we've been arguing a lot more than usual. Is there something that's bothering you?"

Adam: "No, I'm just stressed out from work. It's nothing to worry about."

Evelyn: "Are you sure? I feel like something's not right between us, and I want to work on it together."

Adam: "I appreciate your concern, but really, everything's fine. Let's not worry about it, okay?"

Despite Evelyn's attempts to talk to Adam, he continued to brush off her concerns and assure her that everything was okay. However, Evelyn couldn't shake the feeling that something was amiss in their relationship.

Evelyn started to feel like she was walking on eggshells around Adam. She didn't want to upset him, so she stopped bringing up her concerns and decided to have a moment with Adam.

She called Adam from the living room.

Evelyn: "Adam, I wanted to talk to you about something that's been bothering me."

Adam: "What is it? You know you can tell me anything."

Evelyn: "Well, it's just that I feel like I'm walking on eggshells around you. I don't want to upset you, so I've stopped bringing up my concerns."

Adam: "What do you mean? Why do you feel like you're walking on eggshells?"

Evelyn: "I feel like I can't bring up anything that might be a sensitive topic for you. I don't want to cause an argument or upset you in any way."

Adam: "I see. I'm sorry you feel that way. I don't want you to feel like you can't express your thoughts and feelings around me. We can talk about anything, even if it's something that might be difficult to discuss. Let's work on communicating better and being more open with each other."

But as months went by, Evelyn started to feel like they were growing apart. They had stopped doing the things they used to love, and there was a lack of intimacy between them.

One day, Evelyn arrived home early from work and noticed that Adam was on the phone. As she approached, she could hear snippets of their conversation.

Adam: *"Yes, I understand. It's been a while since we last spoke."*

Evelyn's heart skipped a beat. Who was he talking to?

Adam: *"I've been busy, but I think about you all the time."*

Evelyn's unease grew.

Adam: *"I miss you too."*

Evelyn's stomach tightened. Who was this woman he was talking to?

Adam: *"No, no. Evelyn doesn't suspect a thing. She's been busy with work lately."*

Evelyn's eyes widened. Was he talking about her?

Adam: *"I'll figure out a way to see you soon. I can't wait."*

Evelyn's worst fears were confirmed. She quietly stepped away, unsure of what to do next.

She tried to talk to Adam about it, but he got defensive and accused her of not trusting him. Evelyn felt hurt and confused. She thought they had a strong foundation of trust in their marriage.

As time went on, Evelyn started to notice that their relationship wasn't as perfect as she thought it was. She felt like they were drifting apart, and there was a growing distance between them. She didn't know what to do or how to fix it.

Two

The First Sign

The first sign that something was wrong was when Adam started to spend more time at work than at home. Evelyn didn't mind at first because she understood that he was trying to build his career, but it soon became clear that his work was more important to him than his marriage.

* * *

Evelyn tried to ignore the growing distance between her and Adam, hoping that things would get better with time. But the first sign that something was wrong came when Adam started to spend more time at work than at home.

At first, Evelyn didn't mind. She understood that Adam was trying to build his career and that he was passionate about his work. She wanted to support him in any way she could, so she encouraged him to pursue his dreams.

But as days turned into weeks, and weeks turned into months, Evelyn was starting to feel neglected, like she was playing second fiddle to Adam's career. He would frequently come home late from work, exhausted, and often had no time or energy left for her.

One evening, Evelyn tried to talk to him about it. *"Adam, I feel like we don't spend enough time together. Your work is consuming all your time and energy, and I'm feeling neglected,"* she said.

Adam replied, *"I'm sorry, Evelyn. Work has been really busy lately, and I've been putting in extra hours to meet some deadlines. But things will settle down soon, and we'll have more time together."*

Days went by, and Adam's work continued to consume all his time and energy. Evelyn tried to bring it up again, *"Adam, we need to talk. It feels like your job is taking over your life. I miss spending time with you, and I'm feeling lonely."*

Adam replied, *"I know it feels that way, Evelyn, but my job is very demanding, and I can't just neglect it. But I'll try to make more time for you, I promise."*

Despite Adam's promise, things didn't improve, and Evelyn felt more and more like she was playing second fiddle to his career. She tried to talk to him about it one last time, *"Adam, I can't keep feeling like this. I need you to make time for me and our relationship. I can't keep feeling like I'm not a priority in your life."*

Evelyn couldn't shake off the feeling that she was losing her husband to his job. She missed the long conversations they used to have, where they would discuss everything under the sun, the way they used to laugh together, and the little things that made their relationship special, like cuddling on the couch while watching their favorite show.

Every time Adam came home late and exhausted, Evelyn's heart sank a little more. She longed for the days when they would spend hours talking and laughing, and the thought of losing those moments forever made her feel sad and helpless.

She started to feel resentful and angry towards Adam. She couldn't understand why he was putting his work before their marriage, and it was starting to take a toll on their relationship.

Evelyn took a deep breath and mustered up the courage to address the elephant in the room. She had been feeling neglected by her husband's long working hours for quite some time now, and tonight she couldn't take it anymore.

"Adam, we need to talk," she said as she sat down across from him.

Adam looked up from his laptop and gave her an apologetic smile. "I'm sorry I'm late again. It's just that the project I'm working on is taking up a lot of my time."

"I know," Evelyn replied, her tone serious. "But your constant absence is taking a toll on our marriage. I feel like I'm not a part of your life anymore."

Adam's smile faded, and he sat up straighter in his chair. "What are you talking about? Of course, you're a part of my life. You're my wife."

"But I don't feel like it," Evelyn said, her voice cracking with emotion. "I feel like you're always too busy for me. We barely talk anymore, and when we do, it's about your work."

Adam sighed and rubbed his face tiredly. "I understand where you're coming from, but you have to know that I'm doing this for us. I want to build a better future for us, and that takes a lot of hard work and dedication."

"I know that," Evelyn said, her voice softening. "But I want to be a part of that future. I want us to build it together."

Adam nodded slowly, and a small smile crept onto his face. He listened to her, but he didn't seem to understand the gravity of the situation. "I see what you mean. I've been so focused on my work that I haven't been paying enough attention to you. I'm sorry, Evelyn. I'll try to do better."

Evelyn smiled back at him, feeling a weight lifted off her shoulders. "Thank you, Adam. That's all I wanted to hear.".

But days turned into weeks, and weeks turned into months, and Adam's workaholic tendencies only seemed to get worse. Evelyn felt like she was living with a stranger, someone who didn't care about her or their marriage.

It became clear that Adam's work was more important to him than his marriage. Evelyn didn't know what to do or how to fix it. She felt like she was losing the man she loved to his career, and it was tearing her apart.

Three

The Second Sign

The second sign was when Adam stopped paying attention to Evelyn's needs. He would come home late, exhausted, and not even ask her how her day was. Evelyn tried to talk to him about it, but he brushed her off, saying that he had too much on his plate.

* * *

The second sign that something was wrong in their marriage was when Adam stopped paying attention to Evelyn's needs. He would come home late from work, exhausted, and not even bother to ask her how her day was.

Evelyn tried to talk to him about it, but he would always brush her off, saying that he had too much on his plate. She felt like she was invisible to him, like her feelings and needs didn't matter anymore.

Despite her efforts, Evelyn couldn't seem to connect with her husband. She had hoped that by cooking his favorite meals, they could share some quality time together and talk about their days, but Adam's lack of interest was disheartening.

One evening, after a long day at work, Evelyn had prepared a delicious meal that Adam had been looking forward to all day. But when he finally came home, he barely touched his plate and instead went straight to his laptop.

Evelyn tried to start a conversation, but Adam was too tired to engage. She could tell that he was stressed and preoccupied with work, and it made her feel even more disconnected from him.

As the days went on, Evelyn began to feel like she was losing her husband to his work. She knew that he was working hard to provide for them, but she couldn't help feeling like she was being left behind.

It was like they were living in two separate worlds, with no connection between them.

Evelyn tried to remind herself of the love they shared and how happy they used to be. She hoped that things would get better, but the distance between them only seemed to grow wider with each passing day.

Evelyn's sense of loneliness and isolation only grew as time went on. Despite her attempts to communicate with Adam, he seemed distant and uninterested in their relationship. She felt like she was carrying the weight of their marriage alone, and it was taking a toll on her mental health.

It seemed like no matter what she did, she couldn't get through to him. She tried to plan date nights, surprise him with thoughtful gestures, and even suggested couples therapy, but nothing seemed to make a difference.

Evelyn felt like she was running out of options. She loved Adam, but she couldn't continue living in a marriage where she felt so alone and unimportant. She started to wonder if it was time to consider separation or divorce.

One day, Evelyn decided to take matters into her own hands. She made plans for a romantic date night, hoping that it would bring them closer together.

But when Adam came home, he barely acknowledged her efforts. He was too preoccupied with work, and he didn't seem to care about spending quality time with his wife.

Evelyn felt crushed. She had put so much effort into trying to salvage their marriage, but it seemed like Adam didn't even notice.

She tried to talk to him about it, but he just told her that he had too much on his plate. It was like he didn't even care that he was pushing her away.

Evelyn realized that she couldn't keep living like this. She deserved someone who would love and cherish her, someone who would put her needs first.

She knew that it was time to have a serious conversation with Adam, one where they would have to confront the issues in their marriage head-on. She just hoped that it wasn't too late to save what they had.

Evelyn knew that she couldn't continue living like this. She couldn't keep feeling neglected and unimportant in her own marriage. She decided to have a heart-to-heart conversation with Adam.

One evening, as they sat together in their living room, Evelyn took a deep breath and asked Adam to sit down with her. She knew it was time to have a difficult conversation, but she didn't know how he would react.

"Adam, I need to talk to you about something," she said, looking into his eyes. "I don't know how to say this, but I feel like our marriage is falling apart. I feel like we're drifting further and further apart, and I don't know how to fix it."

Adam was taken aback by her words. He had been so focused on work and his own stress that he hadn't realized how much he had been neglecting his wife. He listened as she poured out her heart, her words cutting through the silence like a knife.

"I'm so sorry, Evelyn," he said, his voice soft and contrite. "I had no idea you were feeling this way. I've been so wrapped up in my job that I haven't been paying attention to you."

He apologized for his behavior and promised to make an effort to be more present in their marriage. He said that he had been so focused on his work that he had forgotten about the most important thing in his life: his wife.

Evelyn was relieved to hear Adam's words. She had been scared that he would brush her off again, but he seemed to genuinely want to fix things between them.

They spent the rest of the evening talking about their feelings and what they needed from each other. It was the first honest conversation they had had in a long time, and it felt like a weight had been lifted off their shoulders.

Evelyn went to bed that night feeling hopeful. Maybe their marriage wasn't doomed after all. Maybe they could work through their issues and come out stronger on the other side.

But as the days went by, Evelyn realized that Adam's promises were just words. He would make an effort for a day or two, but then he would fall back into his old habits.

He would come home late, exhausted, and not even bother to ask her how her day was. He would spend weekends working instead of spending time with her. It was like he had forgotten their heart-to-heart conversation.

Evelyn felt like she had been fooled again. She had allowed herself to hope, only to be let down once more. She started to wonder if their marriage was really salvageable.

It was like they were back to square one. The distance between them was growing wider, and Evelyn didn't know how to bridge the gap.

She tried to talk to Adam again, but he didn't seem to understand how much his behavior was hurting her. He would apologize and promise to do better, but then he would go back to his old ways.

Evelyn knew that she couldn't keep living like this. She needed to take a break from their marriage and figure out what she wanted.

It was time for her to focus on herself and her own needs. She needed to rediscover who she was outside of her marriage and figure out what she wanted from life.

Evelyn knew that it wouldn't be easy, but she was determined to fight for her own happiness, even if it meant leaving her marriage behind.

Four

The Third Sign

The third sign was when Adam started to criticize Evelyn for everything she did. He would nitpick about how she cooked, how she dressed, and even how she cleaned the house. Evelyn started to feel like she couldn't do anything right.

* * *

Evelyn found it difficult to come to terms with the drastic changes in Adam's behavior towards her. He was once a caring and encouraging partner, but now his attitude was often harsh and critical. Evelyn tried to understand the reason for his change, but she couldn't pinpoint anything specific.

One day, while they were having dinner, Adam criticized Evelyn for her cooking. "*This food is tasteless, Evelyn. I can't eat this. I don't understand why you bother cooking when you can't even do it properly.*"

Evelyn felt hurt and confused by Adam's harsh words. "*What's wrong, Adam? I tried my best to cook a decent meal for us.*"

Adam shrugged. "*Your best is not good enough. You should have done better.*"

This type of behavior from Adam became more frequent. For instance, he would belittle her for making minor mistakes or question her abilities in handling certain tasks. The constant criticism began to wear Evelyn down, and she felt like she was walking on eggshells around him.

At first, Evelyn tried to ignore Adam's comments. She thought that maybe he was just having a bad day or was stressed from work. But the criticism didn't stop.

Adam would find fault with everything Evelyn did. He would tell her that her cooking was terrible and that she dressed like an old lady. He would complain about the state of the house and say that she wasn't doing enough to keep it clean.

Evelyn tried to take Adam's criticism constructively and improve herself, but nothing seemed to be good enough. No matter what she did, he would always find something to complain about.

The constant criticism was starting to take a toll on Evelyn's self-esteem. She started to feel like she couldn't do anything right. She felt like she was failing at everything, including her marriage.

She tried to talk to Adam about how his criticism was making her feel, but he didn't seem to care. He told her that he was just trying to help her improve, and that she was being too sensitive.

But Evelyn knew that his criticism wasn't helpful. It was hurtful and was making her doubt herself. She started to avoid doing things that she knew Adam would criticize her for, which only made her feel more trapped.

Evelyn started to withdraw from Adam. She didn't want to be around him because she knew that he would find something to criticize. She started to spend more time on her own, trying to rebuild her self-confidence.

As she spent more time alone, Evelyn started to realize that she had lost sight of who she was. She had spent so much time trying to please Adam that she had forgotten about her own needs and desires.

She started to think about what she wanted from life and what would make her happy. She realized that she didn't want to spend the rest of her life feeling trapped and criticized.

Evelyn knew that she needed to stand up for herself and her own happiness. She couldn't let Adam's criticism control her life.

She started to push back when he criticized her, telling him that his comments were hurtful and that she didn't appreciate them. She also started to communicate more clearly about her needs and expectations in their relationship.

For example, when Adam criticized her for not doing something the way he wanted, she responded firmly, *"Adam, I understand that you have a different way of doing things, but I need you to respect my way of doing them. Your constant criticism is not helpful and it's hurting our relationship."*

She also started to tell him what she needed from him, such as more emotional support and affirmation. *"Adam, I need you to be more supportive of me and my efforts. I appreciate your feedback, but I also need you to be kind and encouraging, especially when I'm feeling down."*

At first, Adam was resistant to these changes in their relationship dynamic, but he gradually started to listen to Evelyn and respect her boundaries.

Adam didn't like this new version of Evelyn. He wanted her to be the quiet, subservient wife that he had married. He didn't want her to have her own opinions or desires.

But Evelyn wasn't willing to go back to the way things were. She was determined to fight for her own happiness, even if it meant standing up to Adam.

Evelyn realized that in addition to setting boundaries and communicating her needs, she also needed to focus on improving her own life and building her confidence. She started taking cooking classes to improve her culinary skills, which not only helped her in the kitchen but also gave her a sense of accomplishment and pride.

She also started paying more attention to her personal style, dressing in a way that made her feel confident and happy. She experimented with different outfits and accessories, and started to embrace her unique sense of fashion.

As Evelyn began to focus on her own growth and self-improvement, she found that she was no longer as affected by Adam's criticism. She had developed a stronger sense of self-worth and confidence, and was able to brush off his negative comments more easily.

She started to take pride in her home and started cleaning it on her own terms, not according to Adam's demands.

But no matter what she did, Adam continued to criticize her. Evelyn started to feel like she couldn't do anything right, no matter how hard she tried.

She knew that she couldn't continue living like this. She needed to find a way out of her marriage and start over. She needed to find a way to be happy on her own terms.

Five

The Breaking Point

> *The breaking point came when Evelyn found out that Adam had been having an affair with a co-worker. She was devastated and didn't know what to do.*

* * *

Evelyn's world came crashing down when she found out that Adam had been having an affair with a co-worker.

Evelyn's heart sank as she watched the video clips her friend had sent her. In disbelief, she saw her husband Adam with his co-worker. She couldn't believe that he would do something like this to her, especially after all the work they had done to improve their relationship.

Feeling like she had been punched in the stomach, Evelyn struggled to catch her breath. She felt like her whole world had come crashing down around her. All the progress they had made, all the love and trust they had built together, seemed to have been shattered in an instant.

Days turned into weeks, and Evelyn was consumed by her thoughts and emotions. She felt like she was living in a fog, unable to focus on anything but the pain and betrayal she was feeling. She couldn't eat, she couldn't sleep, and she could barely function.

One night, she reached her breaking point. She was lying in bed, staring at the ceiling, when she suddenly felt like she couldn't breathe. She was gasping for air, her heart pounding in her chest, and she knew that something was seriously wrong.

Evelyn was feeling overwhelmed and anxious, and before she knew it, she was struggling to catch her breath. She called her friend Karen, who answered the phone with concern in her voice.

"Evelyn, what's going on?" Karen asked.

"I don't know," Evelyn said, trying to steady her breathing. *"I can't catch my breath. I feel like something's wrong."*

Karen didn't waste any time. *"I'm on my way over right now. Just breathe, okay? I'm coming."*

True to her word, Karen arrived at Evelyn's house within minutes. She drove her friend to the hospital, holding her hand the whole way and offering words of reassurance.

At the hospital, the doctors ran tests and determined that Evelyn had had a panic attack, most likely brought on by the stress and anxiety she had been experiencing.

Karen stayed by her side the whole time, providing comfort and support. *"I'm here for you, Evelyn,"* she said. *"We'll get through this together."*

Evelyn felt grateful for Karen's presence and knew that she wouldn't have been able to make it through the ordeal without her. As she took deep breaths and tried to calm her racing thoughts, she knew that she had a friend in Karen who would always be there for her.

How could Adam do this to her? How could he be so selfish and callous? How could he throw away everything they had built together for a cheap fling with a co-worker?

But Evelyn knew the truth. She couldn't ignore the evidence right in front of her. She felt lost and alone, unsure of what to do next. The pain was overwhelming, and she wasn't sure how she would ever be able to trust anyone again.

She spent the next few days in a haze, not sure what to do. She didn't want to throw away her marriage, but she also didn't know how to move forward. She didn't know if she could ever trust Adam again.

Evelyn confided in her close friend Karen about the struggles she was facing in her marriage with Adam. Karen listened attentively and offered her support, but she also suggested something that made Evelyn feel uneasy.

"Have you considered talking to Adam's parents about this?" Karen asked gently.

Evelyn hesitated, unsure about involving Adam's parents in their marital issues. "I don't know," she said uncertainly. "I don't want to cause any drama or make things worse."

Karen nodded understandingly. "I get it. But sometimes, it can be helpful to have an outside perspective. And if anyone knows Adam well, it's his parents. They might be able to offer some insight or advice that could help you."

She thought about it for a moment before finally deciding against it. "I don't think that's a good idea," she said to her friend. "I've never had much of a relationship with them, and I don't want to burden them with our problems."

Karen nodded understandingly. "I get it," she said. "It's just that sometimes, talking to someone who knows both of you can help."

Six

The Decision

After much deliberation, Evelyn decided to confront Adam about the affair. She gave him an ultimatum: either end the affair and work on their marriage, or get a divorce.

* * *

For the next few days, Evelyn was in a state of constant turmoil. She didn't know what to do. She loved Adam, but she couldn't tolerate the betrayal. Finally, after much deliberation, she made a decision.

Evelyn knew that she had to confront Adam about the affair and make a choice. She knew that she couldn't continue living like this, and she needed to make a stand. She mustered up the courage to tell Adam her ultimatum.

Evelyn took a deep breath and looked straight into Adam's eyes. *"I need to talk to you,"* she said, her voice firm.

Adam looked up from his phone and saw the seriousness in her eyes. *"Sure, what's going on?"*

"Eve, what's wrong?" he asked, concerned.

As she spoke, Evelyn felt a weight lifted off her chest. *"Adam, I love* you and I want to work on our marriage," she said. "But I can't do it if you continue the affair. It's either end the affair and work on our marriage, or get a divorce."

Adam's eyes widened as he realized the gravity of the situation. "Evelyn, I'm so sorry. I didn't realize how much this was hurting you," he said, his voice filled with regret.

"You should have thought about that before you started the affair," Evelyn said, her voice tinged with anger. "I can't continue living like this. I need to know that you're committed to our marriage."

Adam looked down at his feet, feeling ashamed. "You're right. I've been selfish and I'm sorry. I will end the affair and do whatever it takes to make things right between us," he said, his voice sincere.

Evelyn nodded, feeling a glimmer of hope. "I want to believe you, Adam. But you need to prove to me that you're serious about saving our marriage," she said, her eyes searching his face.

Adam sat in stunned silence as Evelyn issued her ultimatum. He felt the weight of his mistake bearing down on him, and the fear of losing her was almost suffocating.

"Evelyn, I am so sorry," Adam finally managed to say. "I know that I've messed up and hurt you, but I promise that I will end the affair and work on our marriage. I love you, and I don't want to lose you."

Evelyn looked at him with a mixture of anger and sadness. "How can I trust you, Adam? You've lied to me and betrayed me. I don't know if I can ever forgive you for this."

Adam hung his head in shame. "I understand that it will take time to earn back your trust, but I am willing to do whatever it takes. Please don't give up on us."

Evelyn shook her head. "I need some time to think about this, Adam. I need to figure out if I can ever trust you again."

Adam nodded, feeling the weight of uncertainty settling in his chest. He knew that he had to give her space, but the thought of losing her was almost too much to bear. "I understand, Evelyn. Please know that I am willing to do whatever it takes to make things right."

Evelyn stood up, her eyes full of tears. *"I need some time alone, Adam. Please leave."*

Adam nodded, his heart breaking as he left the room. He knew that he had a long road ahead of him, but he was determined to do whatever it takes to save his marriage.

For the next few weeks, Evelyn and Adam went to couple's therapy to work on their issues. It was a slow process, but they made progress. Adam was more attentive, and he made an effort to show Evelyn how much he loved her.

Evelyn still had her doubts, though. She was afraid that Adam would slip back into his old ways, and she would be hurt again. She didn't want to give up on their marriage, but she didn't want to be a fool either.

In the end, Evelyn decided to give Adam another chance. She could see that he was making an effort, and she loved him enough to try again. It wasn't easy, but they were determined to make it work.

As time went on, Evelyn and Adam's marriage started to heal. They had their ups and downs, but they worked through them together. Evelyn learned to trust Adam again, and he learned to appreciate her more. They were far from perfect, but they were happy.

Looking back, Evelyn realized that the affair was a wake-up call for both of them. It made them realize how much they loved each other and how much they were willing to fight for their marriage. She was grateful for the second chance, and she knew that they would never take each other for granted again.

Seven

The Apology

Adam apologized and promised to end the affair. Evelyn was hesitant to believe him, but she decided to give him another chance.

* * *

Adam approached Evelyn with a sincere expression on his face and began to speak, "I'm so sorry for what I did, Evelyn. I understand that I've hurt you deeply, and I promise to do everything in my power to make things right between us. I know that I've broken your trust, and that's something I deeply regret."

Evelyn looked at him with a mix of hurt and confusion. "I don't know if I can believe you, Adam. How could you do something like that to me?"

Adam took a deep breath and replied, "I know I messed up, and I'm willing to do whatever it takes to earn back your trust. I want to work on our marriage and make things right between us."

Evelyn considered his words for a moment before responding, "I want to believe you, Adam. But I need to see some real effort on your part before I can fully trust you again."

Adam nodded understandingly. "I completely understand, Evelyn. I'm willing to do whatever it takes to prove to you that I'm truly sorry and that I'm committed to making things right between us."

Evelyn took a deep breath and said, "Okay, let's work on our marriage. But you need to understand that it's going to take time and effort from both of us to rebuild what we had before."

Adam nodded in agreement. "I understand, Evelyn. I'm willing to put in the work to make things right between us. Thank you for giving me another chance."

Adam demonstrated his unwavering dedication to their relationship in the following weeks. He made a conscious effort to come home earlier from work, which allowed him to spend more quality time with Evelyn. They would often have long conversations about their day, their future plans, and anything else that was on their minds.

Adam also made a conscious effort to show Evelyn more affection. He would surprise her with small gestures of love, such as leaving her notes around the house, giving her a heartfelt compliment, or holding her hand as they walked down the street.

One evening, Adam surprised Evelyn with a romantic dinner at their favorite restaurant. As they sat down to eat, they talked about how much they appreciated each other and how grateful they were to have found one another. Evelyn was touched by Adam's efforts to make their relationship stronger, and she felt more in love with him than ever before.

"I just want you to know how much you mean to me," Adam said, taking Evelyn's hand across the table. "I know I haven't always been the best partner, but I'm committed to making things work between us. I love you more than anything in this world."

Evelyn's heart swelled with love as she looked into Adam's eyes. "I love you too, Adam," she replied. "I appreciate everything you're doing for us, and I promise to do my part to make our relationship thrive."

Evelyn appreciated Adam's effort, but she was still wary of him. She couldn't help but wonder if he was only doing these things to appease her or if he truly loved her. She decided to talk to a therapist to help her sort through her feelings.

In therapy, Evelyn learned that her trust had been broken and that it would take time and effort to rebuild it. The therapist encouraged her to communicate her feelings to Adam and to establish boundaries that would help her feel safe and secure in the relationship.

Evelyn took her therapist's advice and decided to have an honest conversation with Adam about something that had been bothering her. She took a deep breath before sitting down with Adam to begin their conversation.

"Adam," she started, "there's something I need to talk to you about. It's been weighing on me for a while now, and I think it's important that we address it." Adam's expression showed that he was ready to listen, so Evelyn continued.

Evelyn paused for a moment, her thoughts swirling in her head, before finally mustering the courage to speak. "Adam, we need to talk. Your actions have caused me a lot of pain, and I don't think you even realize it."

Adam's eyes widened as he realized the gravity of the situation. "What do you mean, Evelyn? What have I done?"

"You've hurt me, Adam. You promised me that you would always be there for me, but when I needed you the most, you were nowhere to be found," Evelyn explained, her voice shaking slightly.

Adam's expression softened, and he reached out to take her hand. "I'm sorry, Evelyn. I never meant to hurt you. I know that I haven't been there for you lately, but I want to make it right."

Evelyn nodded, appreciating his apology but still needing to express her feelings. "I know you didn't mean to, Adam, but the fact remains that I don't know if I can trust you anymore. I need you to prove to me that you're committed to our relationship and that you won't hurt me again."

Adam nodded in understanding. "I understand, Evelyn, and I promise to do whatever it takes to make things right between us. You mean the world to me, and I never want to lose your trust." Evelyn felt a sense of relief wash over her, grateful that Adam was willing to work on their relationship and regain her trust.

Over time, Adam continued to prove his love and commitment to Evelyn. He apologized when he made mistakes, listened to her concerns, and made an effort to be more present in their marriage. Evelyn could see that he was truly sorry for what he had done and was willing to do whatever it took to make their marriage work.

Finally, Evelyn began to feel like she could trust Adam again. She started to let go of the anger and hurt that she had been holding onto and opened herself up to the possibility of a happy future with him.

In the end, Evelyn decided to give Adam another chance. She believed that he was truly sorry for what he had done and was committed to making their marriage work. She knew that it wouldn't be easy, but she was willing to put in the effort to rebuild their relationship and to create a happy and fulfilling life together.

Eight

The First Step

The first step towards repairing their marriage was for Adam to quit his job and find a new one. Evelyn didn't want him to be around the co-worker who had caused so much damage to their relationship.

* * *

As they sat at the kitchen table, sipping their coffee, Adam took a deep breath and turned to Evelyn. "There's something I need to tell you," he said, his voice serious.

Evelyn looked at him expectantly, sensing that something important was coming. "What is it, Adam?"

"I've been thinking a lot about us, and I've come to the realization that I need to make some changes if we're going to save our marriage," Adam explained, his eyes fixed on hers.

Evelyn's heart leapt with a glimmer of hope, but she remained cautious. "What kind of changes?"

Adam took Evelyn's hand in his and looked deeply into her eyes. "I've been doing a lot of thinking," he said. "And I've come to a decision. I'm going to quit my job."

Evelyn's eyes widened in surprise. *"What? Adam, are you sure? You've been working there for years."*

Adam nodded firmly. *"I'm sure. I know that my job has been a major source of stress for both of us, especially with the issues we've had with my co-worker. I want to show you that I'm ready to do whatever it takes to make things work between us."*

Evelyn felt a lump forming in her throat. She couldn't believe that Adam was willing to make such a sacrifice for their relationship. "Thank you," she said, her voice barely above a whisper. "That means a lot to me."

Adam squeezed her hand gently. "I love you, Evelyn. And I'm willing to do whatever it takes to prove that to you."

Evelyn's eyes widened in surprise, and she struggled to find the words to express what she was feeling. "Adam, are you sure? I don't want you to give up your job just for me."

"I'm sure, Evelyn," Adam replied firmly. "My job isn't as important to me as you are. I want to be here for you, to support you and be a better husband to you. And if that means quitting my job and finding something else here, then that's what I'll do."

Evelyn felt tears prick at the corners of her eyes as she looked at her husband. For the first time in a long time, she felt a glimmer of hope that they could make things work between them. "Thank you, Adam," she whispered, squeezing his hand. "That means more to me than you'll ever know."

Evelyn felt a weight lift off her shoulders as Adam told her he would quit his job. She knew how much he enjoyed it, but she also knew that it was causing a lot of problems in their marriage.

As Adam began to search for a new job, Evelyn offered her support and encouragement. She knew that it wouldn't be easy for him to find something else, especially in a different field. But she also knew that it was important for him to find something that would make him happy and fulfilled.

Over the next few weeks, Adam worked hard to find a new job. He applied to numerous positions and went on several interviews. It was a stressful and challenging time for both of them, but Evelyn did her best to remain positive and supportive.

Finally, after what seemed like an eternity, Adam received an offer from a company in a completely different field. It wasn't exactly what he had been looking for, but it was a start.

To Evelyn's surprise, Adam was excited about the new opportunity. He saw it as a chance to start fresh and try something new. And despite the fact that it would be a significant pay cut, he was willing to take it.

Evelyn was proud of him for taking such a big step, and she knew that it was necessary for their marriage. She hoped that it would be worth it in the long run, and that they would be able to build a stronger, more stable future together.

Evelyn felt a glimmer of hope as she saw Adam taking concrete steps towards repairing their relationship. It was going to be a long road, but she was willing to work hard to get their marriage back on track.

Adam's new job was challenging, but he was determined to prioritize his marriage and make time for Evelyn. He would often surprise her with small gestures of affection, like bringing her coffee in bed or cooking her favorite meal.

Evelyn appreciated these efforts, and she reciprocated by making time for Adam as well. They started to take walks together in the evenings and would spend their weekends doing things that they both enjoyed. It was slow progress, but it was progress nonetheless.

As they spent more time together, Evelyn began to feel a renewed sense of connection with Adam. She could feel herself letting go of the pain and hurt that she had been carrying for so long. They still had a lot of work to do, but for the first time in a long time, Evelyn felt optimistic about their future together.

Adam noticed the change in Evelyn, and it made him even more committed to making their marriage work. He knew that he had caused her a lot of pain, but he was determined to do whatever it took to make things right.

Nine

The Therapy

Evelyn and Adam started to attend therapy sessions to work through their issues. It was difficult at first, but they both wanted to save their marriage.

* * *

One of the things that they did to strengthen their relationship was to have counselling sessions. At first, Adam was reluctant, but he soon realized that it was an important step towards healing their marriage. The sessions helped them communicate better and understand each other's needs.

Evelyn and Adam had both agreed that they needed outside help to work through the challenges in their marriage. They decided to schedule an appointment with the therapist who specialized in helping couples rebuild trust and work through past hurts.

During their first session, the therapist asked them to share their experiences and feelings about what had happened. Evelyn talked about the pain and insecurity she had felt when she found out about

Adam's affair, and Adam expressed his remorse and regret for what he had done.

The therapist listened carefully, and then suggested some exercises they could do to improve their communication and rebuild trust. They were given homework assignments to work on between sessions, such as writing letters to each other expressing their feelings and practicing active listening.

The therapy sessions were emotionally draining, but also incredibly rewarding. They began to see improvements in their relationship, and started to feel hopeful about their future together.

One of the biggest breakthroughs came when they were able to address the underlying issues that had led to Adam's affair. They were able to have an honest and open conversation about their needs and desires, and to find ways to meet those needs within their marriage.

It wasn't always easy, and there were times when they both wanted to give up. But they both knew that they wanted to save their marriage, and they were willing to do whatever it took to make it work.

In one of their counselling sessions, Evelyn hesitantly began to share her feelings with Adam. "I can't stop thinking about what happened, Adam. Your affair has really affected me. I feel so insecure and I don't know how to get over it."

Adam's expression softened as he realized the extent of the damage he had caused. "I'm so sorry, Evelyn. I had no idea that it was affecting you this much. I'll do whatever it takes to help you feel better."

Evelyn took a deep breath and continued. "I just feel so worthless sometimes. Like I'm not enough for you."

Adam reached out and took her hand. "Evelyn, you are more than enough for me. You're everything to me."

Evelyn looked up at him, tears streaming down her face. "How can you say that after what you did?"

Adam took a moment to gather his thoughts before speaking. "I know I messed up, Evelyn. But I promise to do better. I want to show you how much you mean to me."

Over the next few weeks, as Adam continued to put in effort to rebuild their relationship, Evelyn started to feel like herself again. She felt more confident and secure, and she started to let go of the pain and hurt that Adam's affair had caused.

Adam noticed the change in Evelyn and felt relieved that his efforts were paying off. He felt grateful for the second chance that Evelyn had given him and vowed to never take her for granted again.

One evening, as they sat together on the couch, Adam turned to Evelyn and said, "You know, Evelyn, you're amazing. I don't tell you that enough."

Evelyn smiled, feeling a warmth in her chest. "Thank you, Adam. I appreciate it."

"No, really," Adam continued, taking her hand in his. "You're the most incredible person I know. You're beautiful, smart, and so strong. I'm lucky to have you in my life."

Evelyn felt tears welling up in her eyes as she listened to Adam's words. She had never felt so loved and appreciated before. "Thank you, Adam," she said, her voice barely above a whisper.

Adam leaned in and kissed her gently on the lips. "I mean it, Evelyn. You're everything to me."

As they sat there together, wrapped in each other's arms, Evelyn knew that they had a long road ahead of them. But with Adam by her side, she felt like they could overcome anything. They were a team, and they would face whatever challenges came their way together.

Slowly but surely, Evelyn started to feel better about herself. She realized that Adam truly loved her and was committed to making things right. It wasn't easy, but they were both willing to put in the work to rebuild their marriage.

Evelyn began to feel a sense of hope and optimism about their future together. She saw how much effort he was putting into rebuilding their trust and it gave her the courage to start letting her guard down.

They started to go on dates again, taking long walks in the park and spending quality time talking and laughing together. Evelyn felt like they were reconnecting in a way that she had never thought possible.

During one of their walks, Adam turned to her and said, "You know,

Evelyn, I don't want to ever lose you again. I know I messed up, but I'm willing to do whatever it takes to make things right."

Evelyn looked at him, feeling a mixture of emotions. Part of her was still hurt and angry about what had happened, but another part of her wanted to believe that they could overcome it.

"I want to believe you, Adam," she said. "But it's going to take time. I need to be able to trust you again."

"I understand," Adam replied, taking her hand in his. "I'm willing to be patient and work hard to earn your trust back."

Over the next few weeks, Adam continued to show his commitment to their relationship, and Evelyn started to feel like they were making progress. They talked openly and honestly about their feelings, and Adam was always there to listen and support her.

As they sat together on the couch one evening, Evelyn turned to Adam and said, *"Thank you for never giving up on us."*

Adam smiled and took her hand. *"I could never give up on us, Evelyn. You mean everything to me."*

With each passing day, Evelyn felt more and more hopeful about their future together. She knew that they still had a lot of work to do, but she was willing to take things one day at a time, knowing that they were in it together.

Even though there were still moments of doubt and fear, Evelyn felt like they were making progress. She knew that it would take time to fully recover from the affair, but she was willing to take it one day at a time. Adam was also committed to their marriage and was willing to do whatever it takes to make things right.

As time passed, Evelyn started to feel more secure in their relationship. She began to trust Adam again and was grateful for the effort he had put into repairing their marriage. She knew that they still had a long way to go, but she was willing to work on it together.

Despite the progress they had made, Evelyn still struggled with the memory of Adam's affair. She had moments of doubt and insecurity, wondering if he would cheat on her again. However, Adam was patient and understanding, and he reassured her that he was committed to their marriage and would never betray her again.

Evelyn was grateful for the love and support that Adam had shown her. She knew that their marriage would never be the same again, but she believed that they could build a new foundation and create a stronger bond. She was willing to take the risk and fight for their love.

Their marriage was far from perfect, but they had learned to communicate better and support each other. They were more committed than ever to each other, and their love had grown deeper and stronger. Evelyn knew that they still had work to do, but she was confident that they could overcome any obstacle together.

As time went on, they continued to attend therapy sessions, and they also started to work on their own individual issues. They both realized that they had contributed to the problems in their marriage, and that they needed to work on themselves in order to be better partners.

It was a long and challenging process, but Evelyn and Adam were committed to making it work. They both knew that they still had a lot of work to do, but they were making progress, and that was what mattered.

Eventually, they both started to see the benefits of therapy. They were able to communicate more openly and honestly with each other, and they were able to rebuild the trust that had been lost. They started to feel like they were on the same team again, and that they could face anything together.

It was difficult at first, but they both wanted to save their marriage. They knew that it wouldn't be easy, but they were willing to put in the work to make it happen.

Ten

The Progress

Slowly but surely, Evelyn and Adam started to make progress in their therapy sessions. They learned how to communicate better and how to understand each other's needs.

Evelyn and Adam continued to attend therapy sessions and work on their marriage. It was a slow process, but they were both committed to making things work.

In the beginning, it was difficult to open up to each other and talk about their feelings. But with the help of their therapist, they learned how to communicate in a way that was respectful and understanding.

During one of their conversations, Evelyn was taken aback when Adam confided in her that he had been feeling neglected and unappreciated for a long time. He had been working tirelessly to provide for their family, but he didn't feel like he had any time for himself.

Evelyn felt guilty for not realizing the extent of Adam's struggles earlier. She had been so consumed by her own pain and insecurities that she hadn't paid enough attention to what he was going through. She listened patiently as Adam opened up about how he was feeling, and she vowed to make a conscious effort to be more supportive.

Together, they came up with a plan to help Adam find more balance in his life. Evelyn encouraged him to pursue his hobbies and to take breaks when he needed to. They also started to prioritize their time together as a couple, making sure to schedule date nights and weekends away from the stresses of work and home life.

Over time, Adam began to feel more fulfilled and energized. He still worked hard to provide for their family, but he also made time for the things that he enjoyed. This newfound sense of balance made a world of difference in their marriage, and Evelyn was grateful to see Adam thriving once again.

Their conversations became more open and honest, and they made a conscious effort to be more attentive to each other's needs. As they worked together to rebuild their relationship, Evelyn and Adam felt a renewed sense of connection and commitment to each other.

Adam, in turn, was surprised to learn how much his criticism and absence had hurt Evelyn. He didn't realize how much she had been struggling to hold things together on her own.

As they continued to work through their issues, Evelyn and Adam started to make progress. They learned how to listen to each other without getting defensive and how to express their needs in a way that was constructive.

They started to spend more time together and make an effort to do things that they both enjoyed. They went on date nights, took long walks together, and even started to plan a vacation.

Evelyn was grateful for the progress they had made, but she knew that there was still a long way to go. She was still hurt by Adam's affair and struggled to trust him again.

Adam was patient and understanding, and he continued to work hard to show Evelyn how much he loved and appreciated her. He wrote her love letters, cooked her favorite meals, and made sure to tell her how much she meant to him every day.

Despite the progress they had made, there were still moments of doubt and fear. Evelyn couldn't help but wonder if Adam would cheat again, and Adam worried that he would never be able to fully regain her trust.

But they both knew that they wanted to be together and were willing to do whatever it took to make their marriage work. They continued to attend therapy and put in the hard work necessary to rebuild their relationship.

It wasn't easy, but they were making progress. They learned how to communicate better and how to understand each other's needs. They were more in love than they had been in a long time, and they were hopeful about the future.

As they completed all their therapy sessions. Evelyn knew that they still had a long road ahead of them, but she was confident that they could make it work. They had come so far, and they weren't about to give up now. They were determined to fight for their love and their marriage. They had come too far to give up now. They were in this together, for better or for worse. They were a team, and they were stronger together than they ever could be apart.

Eleven

The Setback

However, there were still setbacks along the way. Adam would sometimes slip back into old habits, and Evelyn would get frustrated and angry.

* * *

Evelyn and Adam had made progress in their therapy sessions, but it wasn't a smooth journey. There were still times when Adam would slip back into old habits, and Evelyn would get frustrated and angry.

Evelyn was looking forward to celebrating their wedding anniversary with Adam, but as the day approached, she couldn't shake the feeling that something was off. When the day finally arrived, she eagerly awaited Adam's call, but it never came. She tried to push the disappointment aside and focus on preparing a special dinner for the two of them. However, when Adam finally came home, he was exhausted from work and barely acknowledged the occasion.

Evelyn tried to hide her disappointment, but Adam could sense that something was wrong. *"Is everything okay?"* he asked tentatively. Evelyn's voice was barely above a whisper as she responded, *"You forgot, didn't you?"* Adam's face fell as he realized his mistake. *"I'm so sorry, Evelyn,"* he said, *"I've been so caught up with work that I completely lost track of time."* Evelyn's eyes welled up with tears, *"It's not just about forgetting the date,"* she said, *"It's about feeling unimportant to you. It feels like you don't value our relationship."*

Adam knew he had let her down, and he was determined to make it right. *"I understand how you feel,"* he said, *"and I promise to make it up to you. Let's make plans to celebrate properly this weekend, just the two of us."* Evelyn's expression softened at Adam's words, and she nodded slowly. *"Okay,"* she said, *"I'd like that."*

Another setback happened when Adam started to spend more time with his friends than with her. He would go out drinking with them and come home late, sometimes not even calling to let her know where he was.

Evelyn tried to talk to him about it, but Adam would brush it off and say that he needed to relax and have some fun. This made Evelyn feel like she wasn't a priority in his life.

Another setback occurred when Evelyn discovered that Adam had lied to her about something insignificant. Even though it was a small thing, it shattered her trust in him, and she found it hard to forgive him.

During their therapy sessions, they learned that setbacks were a natural part of the healing process. It wasn't always going to be smooth sailing, but it was important to keep moving forward.

Evelyn and Adam had to learn how to communicate effectively and be honest with each other. They had to set boundaries and learn how to respect each other's feelings.

Evelyn had to learn how to let go of her anger and forgive Adam for his mistakes. It wasn't easy, but she knew that holding onto resentment would only hurt their relationship.

Adam had to learn how to prioritize his marriage and make Evelyn feel loved and appreciated. He had to show her that she was his number one priority, and he was willing to make sacrifices for their relationship.

Together, they worked through their setbacks and made progress.

They were committed to each other and their marriage, and they refused to give up.

Even though there were still tough times ahead, they knew that they could face them together. They were in this for the long haul, and they were determined to make it work.

Twelve

The Support System

Evelyn started to lean on her friends and family for support. They helped her through the tough times and encouraged her to keep fighting for her marriage.

* * *

Evelyn felt grateful for the support system she had in her life. Her friends and family were always there for her, ready to listen and offer advice. They knew how much she loved Adam and wanted to see her marriage work out.

Whenever Evelyn felt down or discouraged, she would call her best friend, Karen. Karen had been through a tough divorce herself and knew exactly what Evelyn was going through. She would offer words of wisdom and encouragement, telling Evelyn to keep fighting for her marriage.

Evelyn's parents were also a huge source of support. They had been married for over 40 years and knew that marriage was hard work. They would often invite Evelyn and Adam over for dinner, hoping to give them a chance to reconnect and talk things out.

Evelyn's sister, Samantha, was another person she leaned on. Samantha had always been the protective older sister, and she was fiercely loyal to Evelyn. She would listen to Evelyn vent and offer a shoulder to cry on when things got tough.

Even some of Evelyn's co-workers became part of her support system. They would invite her out for drinks after work, or send her encouraging messages throughout the day. Knowing that she had people in her corner helped Evelyn to stay strong and keep fighting for her marriage.

Of course, there were times when Evelyn felt like giving up. She was tired of the constant arguing and the feeling of uncertainty. But whenever those thoughts crept in, her support system was there to remind her of why she started fighting for her marriage in the first place.

They reminded her of the good times, the love that she and Adam shared, and the potential for a brighter future. They helped her to see that it was worth the struggle and the hard work.

Through it all, Evelyn remained grateful for the people in her life who never gave up on her. They helped her through the tough times and encouraged her to keep fighting for her marriage.

Thirteen

The Doubts

> *Despite the progress they had made, Evelyn still had doubts about whether or not their marriage would survive. She didn't want to go through the pain of another affair.*

* * *

Evelyn tried to push her doubts aside and focus on the progress they had made, but they still lingered in the back of her mind. She couldn't help but wonder if Adam was truly committed to their marriage or if he would slip back into old habits.

The fear of another affair haunted her, and she started to become paranoid about Adam's every move. She would check his phone, email, and social media accounts to make sure he wasn't communicating with anyone he shouldn't be.

Evelyn knew that this behavior wasn't healthy, but she couldn't help herself. The pain of betrayal was still fresh in her mind, and she didn't want to be blindsided again.

Adam noticed Evelyn's behavior and tried to reassure her that he was committed to their marriage. He promised that he would never hurt her again and that he would do whatever it takes to make things right between them.

However, despite his promises, Evelyn still found herself doubting him. She couldn't shake the feeling that he was still hiding something from her, and this caused tension between them.

They resumed their therapy sessions and became more intense as they worked through Evelyn's trust issues. The therapist encouraged them to be open and honest with each other, but it was difficult for Evelyn to let her guard down.

As time went on, Evelyn started to realize that her doubts were not only affecting her but also their marriage. She knew that she needed to work through her issues if they were going to move forward.

With the help of her therapist and the support of her loved ones, Evelyn started to open up more to Adam. She allowed herself to be vulnerable and express her fears and doubts.

Adam listened patiently and reassured her that he loved her and was committed to their marriage. He understood why she was feeling the way she was and promised to do everything in his power to regain her trust.

Slowly but surely, Evelyn's doubts began to fade. She started to believe that their marriage could survive and even thrive. She learned to let go of her fears and put her trust in Adam.

It wasn't easy, but they were making progress. Evelyn learned that trust is something that needs to be earned and that it takes time to heal from betrayal.

Despite her doubts, Evelyn was proud of the progress they had made. They had both worked hard to save their marriage, and it was starting to show. She knew that there would be more challenges ahead, but she was ready to face them together with Adam.

She didn't want to go through the pain of another affair, but she was willing to take the risk if it meant saving her marriage. She knew that Adam wasn't perfect, but neither was she. They were both human and made mistakes, but they were committed to working through them together.

Evelyn was grateful for the support system she had and for the progress they had made. She was hopeful for the future and excited to see where their marriage would take them. They still had a long way to go, but they were on the right track.

In the end, Evelyn realized that doubts were a natural part of any relationship, but what mattered was how they were addressed and worked through. She had learned that trust was something that needed to be earned and that it was worth fighting for.

Fourteen

The Reflection

Evelyn started to reflect on her own behavior and how it might have contributed to their marital problems. She realized that she had been too passive and had let Adam take control of their relationship.

* * *

Evelyn spent hours thinking about the problems in her marriage. She knew that it wasn't entirely Adam's fault, and that she had to take responsibility for her own actions. She began to think back on the early days of their relationship and how happy they had been.

As she thought more about it, she realized that she had been too passive in their marriage. She had let Adam take control of everything, and had not spoken up when she disagreed with him. She had always put his needs before her own, and it had led to resentment and unhappiness.

Evelyn started to see that in order to save her marriage, she needed to make changes in herself. She needed to start speaking up and asserting her own needs and desires. She needed to become an equal partner in their relationship.

It was a difficult realization for her, but she knew it was necessary. She started to work on her communication skills and on expressing her feelings in a constructive way. She also began to take more time for herself, doing things that made her happy and fulfilled.

As she made these changes, she started to feel more confident and empowered. She realized that she didn't need Adam to make her happy; she could find happiness within herself. This realization gave her the strength to continue working on her marriage.

She also started to see that Adam was responding positively to her changes. He seemed to respect her more and was more willing to listen to her point of view. It was a small step, but it gave her hope that their marriage could be saved.

Evelyn continued to reflect on her own behavior and how it had affected their relationship. She started to see patterns in her behavior that she had never noticed before. She realized that she had a tendency to avoid conflict, even when it was necessary.

She knew that this was a pattern she needed to break. She started to practice speaking up and confronting issues head-on. It was uncomfortable at first, but it got easier with time.

As she made these changes, she started to feel more in control of her life. She realized that she had the power to change her circumstances and to create the life she wanted.

Despite her doubts and fears, Evelyn was determined to save her marriage. She knew that it would take hard work and sacrifice, but she was willing to do whatever it took. She also knew that she couldn't do it alone; she needed Adam's support and commitment.

She continued to attend therapy sessions with Adam, and they worked together to improve their communication and understanding of each other's needs. It was a slow process, but they were making progress.

Evelyn knew that there were no guarantees in life, and that their marriage might not survive. But she also knew that she had given it her all, and that was all she could do.

As she continued to reflect on her own behavior, she felt more confident in herself and in her ability to create a better future. She knew that whatever happened, she would be okay.

Fifteen

The Changes

Evelyn started to make changes in her own life. She started to stand up for herself and communicate her needs more clearly.

Evelyn realized that if she wanted her marriage to work, she needed to start making changes in her own life. She had always been a passive person, but she knew that she couldn't continue to let Adam take control of their relationship.

So, Evelyn started to make a conscious effort to stand up for herself. She began to communicate her needs more clearly to Adam, and she didn't back down when he disagreed with her. It wasn't easy at first, but with time, she became more confident in herself.

She also started to make changes in other areas of her life. She took up hobbies that she enjoyed, like painting and hiking. She made new friends and started to do things that made her happy, regardless of whether or not Adam wanted to do them too.

These changes helped Evelyn to regain her sense of self-worth. She no longer felt like she was living in Adam's shadow. Instead, she felt like she was her own person with her own identity.

Adam noticed the changes in Evelyn and was impressed by her newfound confidence. He began to treat her with more respect and consideration. He listened to her needs and opinions and was more willing to compromise.

As a result, their marriage started to improve even more. They were communicating better than ever before, and they were both putting in effort to make things work.

Evelyn was proud of the progress they had made, but she also knew that there was still work to be done. She continued to work on herself, to communicate her needs, and to stand up for herself. She knew that it was a never-ending process, but it was worth it to have a healthy and happy marriage.

Overall, the changes that Evelyn made were crucial to the survival of their marriage. She learned that she was capable of standing up for herself and communicating her needs clearly. This, in turn, helped Adam to treat her with more respect and consideration. She started to stand up for herself and communicate her needs more clearly.

Sixteen

The Realization

Evelyn realized that she was strong enough to leave Adam if things didn't work out. She didn't want to be trapped in a loveless marriage.

* * *

Evelyn's realization came as a shock to her. She had never thought about leaving Adam before, but now she knew it was an option. She felt empowered by the thought that she didn't have to stay in a marriage that wasn't fulfilling.

As she thought more about it, she realized that she had been staying with Adam out of fear. Fear of being alone, fear of what others would think, and fear of not being able to make it on her own.

But now, she knew that those fears were holding her back. She started to think about what her life could be like if she left Adam. She could pursue her own interests, make new friends, and maybe even find love again.

The idea of leaving Adam was scary, but it was also liberating. She didn't have to stay in a marriage that wasn't working for her. She could choose her own path in life.

She started to talk to her therapist about her feelings, and the therapist encouraged her to explore her options. She also talked to her friends and family, who supported her decision to do what was best for herself.

As she reflected on her marriage, she realized that it wasn't just Adam's fault. She had played a role in their problems too. She had let Adam take control and hadn't communicated her needs clearly.

But now, she was starting to change that. She was standing up for herself and taking control of her life. She felt more confident and empowered than she had in a long time.

She didn't know what the future held, but she knew that she had options. She didn't have to stay in a loveless marriage if she didn't want to. She could choose a different path and create the life that she wanted.

She felt grateful for the support of her therapist, friends, and family. They had helped her to see that she was strong enough to make her own decisions and take control of her life.

She knew that leaving Adam would be hard, but she was ready for the challenge. She was excited about the possibilities that lay ahead of her and felt optimistic about her future.

She didn't want to be trapped in a loveless marriage, and now she knew that she didn't have to be. She could choose her own path in life and create a future that was fulfilling and rewarding.

As she thought about her decision, she felt a sense of peace wash over her. She knew that it wouldn't be easy, but she also knew that it was the right thing to do. She was ready to take the next step and see where life would take her.

Seventeen

The Reconciliation

After many months of hard work, Evelyn and Adam reconciled. They both felt like they had a deeper understanding of each other and their needs.

* * *

Evelyn and Adam's marriage had gone through a lot of turmoil, but they had finally made it through. They had worked hard to repair their relationship and it had paid off.

Evelyn felt a sense of relief and happiness that they had reconciled. She knew that it had taken a lot of work, but it was worth it. She felt like they had a new start and a chance to build a stronger foundation for their marriage.

Adam also felt relieved that they had reconciled. He had been worried that they wouldn't be able to work things out, but he was glad they had. He felt like he had a deeper appreciation for Evelyn and their marriage.

They both knew that they had to continue working on their relationship, and they were willing to do the work. They felt like they had a better understanding of each other and their needs. They knew that it wouldn't be easy, but they were both committed to making it work.

They continued to attend therapy sessions and work on their communication skills. They knew that they had to be open and honest with each other if their marriage was going to succeed.

They started to do things together again, like going on dates and taking walks in the park. They felt like they had rekindled their love for each other and were excited about their future together.

Evelyn felt like she had grown a lot during their separation. She had become more independent and confident in herself. She knew that she didn't need Adam to make her happy, but that they could be happy together.

Adam also felt like he had grown during their separation. He had learned to appreciate Evelyn more and to not take her for granted. He knew that he had to be a better husband to her if their marriage was going to work.

They both felt like they had a new appreciation for each other and their relationship. They had gone through a tough time, but they had come out the other side stronger and more committed to each other.

Evelyn felt like she could trust Adam again. She knew that he had made mistakes in the past, but she felt like he was committed to their marriage and to making things work.

Adam also felt like he could trust Evelyn again. He knew that she had been hurt by his actions, but he felt like she had forgiven him and was willing to give him another chance.

They both felt like they had a renewed sense of hope for their marriage. They knew that it wouldn't be easy, but they were willing to work at it. They felt like they had a chance to build a better and stronger marriage.

They both knew that there would be setbacks along the way, but they felt more equipped to handle them now. They knew that they could lean on each other and their support system if things got tough.

They both felt like they had a deeper understanding of each other and their needs. They knew that it was important to be open and honest with each other if they wanted their marriage to work.

They both felt like they had come a long way from where they had been. They knew that they had a lot of work ahead of them, but they felt like they were on the right path.

They both felt like they had a deeper appreciation for their marriage and each other. They knew that they had been given a second chance and they weren't going to waste it.

They both felt like they had a deeper understanding of love and commitment. They knew that it wasn't always easy, but it was worth it. They both felt like they had a deeper understanding of each other and their needs.

Eighteen

The Renewed commitment

Evelyn and Adam renewed their commitment to each other and their marriage. They made promises to always communicate openly and honestly with each other, to prioritize their relationship, and to work together to build a future they both wanted.

* * *

Evelyn and Adam had come a long way in repairing their relationship. After the pain and turmoil of the affair, they had worked hard to rebuild their trust and intimacy. They had both been through so much, but they had emerged stronger for it.

Now, they were ready to make a renewed commitment to each other and their marriage. They knew that it wouldn't be easy, but they were determined to make it work. They wanted to create a future together that was based on mutual respect, understanding, and love.

One of the first things they did was to sit down and have an honest conversation about their relationship. They talked about what had gone wrong in the past and how they could avoid making the same mistakes in the future. They both agreed that communication was key and promised to always be open and honest with each other.

They also talked about their goals for the future. They discussed where they wanted to be in 5, 10, and 20 years, both individually and as a couple. They made plans to work together to achieve their shared dreams and support each other in their individual pursuits.

Evelyn and Adam knew that their renewed commitment would require effort and dedication. They committed to going to couples therapy regularly to continue working on their relationship. They also promised to prioritize their marriage above all else, even when life got busy and stressful.

They realized that there would be challenges along the way, but they were prepared to face them together. They promised to work through any issues that arose and to never give up on each other or their marriage.

"We need to make sure we keep the romance alive in our relationship," Evelyn said to Adam one evening over dinner. "I don't want us to fall back into old habits and neglect each other."

Adam nodded in agreement. "I know what you mean. Let's plan date nights and surprises for each other. And we should make a conscious effort to show affection and appreciation on a daily basis. Even small gestures can go a long way in keeping our connection strong."

Evelyn smiled. "That sounds like a great plan. Let's make a commitment to each other to prioritize our relationship and keep the spark alive."

As they moved forward with their renewed commitment, Evelyn and Adam were filled with hope and optimism. They knew that they had been through a lot, but they also knew that they had come out the other side stronger and more in love than ever before.

They were grateful for the support of their friends and family, who had stood by them throughout their journey. They also knew that their renewed commitment would inspire others to work on their own relationships and not give up when things got tough.

Evelyn and Adam looked forward to the future with excitement and anticipation. They knew that there would be ups and downs, but they were confident that they could face anything together. They were committed to building a life full of love, trust, and happiness, and they knew that they had the strength and determination to make it happen.

As they looked into each other's eyes, Evelyn and Adam knew that they had found their forever partner. They held hands and smiled, grateful for the love they shared and the renewed commitment they had made to each other.

Nineteen

The Relapse

> *Despite their renewed commitment, there were still moments when Evelyn and Adam struggled. They would occasionally slip back into old habits and behaviors, causing tension and disagreements.*

* * *

Evelyn and Adam had been through a lot to get to where they were. They had fought hard to save their marriage, and they both wanted it to work. However, despite their best efforts, they still faced challenges along the way.

There were times when Adam would revert to his old ways, and Evelyn would feel like they were right back where they started. It was frustrating for both of them, and it caused tension in their relationship.

Evelyn knew that change wasn't easy, but she sometimes wondered if they would ever truly be able to leave their past behind. She worried that they would always be haunted by the memories of Adam's affair and the pain it had caused.

Adam, on the other hand, was committed to making things work. He knew that he had made mistakes in the past, but he was determined to be a better husband to Evelyn. He tried his best to be patient and understanding, even when Evelyn got angry with him.

They both continued to attend therapy sessions and worked on their communication skills. They tried to be open and honest with each other, and they talked about their feelings regularly.

Despite their efforts, there were still moments when they struggled. They would have disagreements about small things, and it would sometimes escalate into something bigger. They both knew that they needed to work on their ability to handle conflicts in a healthy way.

Sometimes, Evelyn would get frustrated and feel like they were never going to be able to move past their issues. But then Adam would surprise her with a kind gesture or a heartfelt apology, and she would remember why she loved him.

They both acknowledged that their journey towards healing and reconciliation was going to be a long one. There would be setbacks and challenges along the way, but they were committed to each other and their marriage.

Despite their relapses, they both knew that they had come a long way since the affair. They had grown individually and as a couple, and they were both proud of the progress they had made.

They also knew that they needed to continue to put in the effort to make things work. It wasn't going to be easy, but they were both willing to do whatever it takes to save their marriage.

There were times when they would take a step forward, and then two steps back. But they were determined to keep moving forward. They knew that it wasn't going to be a linear path, but they were both willing to ride the ups and downs together.

Despite the relapses and challenges, they both knew that they loved each other deeply. They knew that they had a connection that was worth fighting for.

They continued to work on their relationship, and with time, the relapses became less frequent. They learned how to communicate better and handle conflicts in a healthier way.

It wasn't perfect, but they both knew that they were making

progress. They were both grateful for the love and support that they had received from their friends and family, and they were both committed to making their marriage work.

Even though there were still moments of tension and disagreements, they both knew that they were in a much better place than they had been before. They were both committed to their renewed commitment and were looking forward to building a happy and healthy future together.

Twenty

The Reminder

During these moments, Evelyn would remind herself of the progress they had made and how much they had both invested in their relationship. She refused to give up on their love.

* * *

Evelyn would remind herself of the progress they had made and how much they had both invested in their relationship. She refused to let their hard work go to waste.

Evelyn knew that relationships took work, and that setbacks were a normal part of the process. She had learned the hard way that ignoring problems only made them worse, and that facing them head-on was the only way to move forward.

One day, while they were sitting on the couch together, Evelyn turned to Adam and said, *"You know, I used to be so afraid of conflict. I thought that if we disagreed on something, it meant that our marriage was in trouble. But now I realize that disagreements are normal, and that we can work through them together."*

Adam put his arm around her. *"I feel the same way,"* he said. *"I used to *think that a good marriage was one where there were no problems, but now I know that a good marriage is one where we work together to solve problems."*

Their conversation was a reminder of how much they had grown as individuals and as a couple. They had learned to embrace conflict and to work through their issues together. Evelyn knew that setbacks were a normal part of the process, but she also knew that they had the tools to overcome any obstacle. As long as they faced their problems together, they could continue to build a strong and healthy marriage.

Adam, too, remained committed to their marriage. He was grateful for the chance to make things right and to prove his love and loyalty to Evelyn.

Together, they continued to attend therapy sessions and work on their communication skills. They learned how to navigate disagreements and resolve conflicts in a healthy and productive way.

As they grew stronger as a couple, they also grew stronger as individuals. Evelyn became more confident and assertive, while Adam learned how to listen and empathize.

They both knew that they still had a long way to go, but they were proud of the progress they had made. They felt closer than ever before and were excited about their future together.

Evelyn was grateful for the reminder that their love was worth fighting for. She knew that they would face more challenges along the way, but she was confident that they could overcome anything as long as they stayed committed to each other.

And so they continued on their journey, hand in hand, with the knowledge that their love was stronger than any obstacle they might face.

Twenty-One

The Patience

Evelyn learned that rebuilding a marriage takes time and patience. She had to be patient with herself, with Adam, and with the process.

* * *

Rebuilding a marriage is a slow and delicate process that requires a lot of patience. Evelyn understood this, and she was willing to give it the time and effort it deserved. She knew that she couldn't expect everything to be perfect right away, and that setbacks were inevitable.

In their therapy sessions, Evelyn and Adam had learned that it was important to be patient with each other, to listen and try to understand each other's point of view. Evelyn had to remind herself of this every time she felt frustrated or disappointed. She knew that she couldn't force Adam to change overnight, and that she had to be patient with his progress.

There were still moments when they would argue or misunderstand each other. But Evelyn had learned to take a step back, to breathe and think before reacting. She had also learned to communicate her feelings in a calm and respectful way, instead of getting angry or defensive.

Adam had also shown a lot of patience and understanding during their journey of rebuilding their marriage. He had been willing to listen to Evelyn's needs and concerns, and had made an effort to change his behavior. He knew that it wouldn't be easy, but he was committed to making their marriage work.

Evelyn had also learned to be patient with herself. She had to let go of the guilt and shame she felt about her role in their marital problems. She had to accept that she couldn't change the past, but she could work on being a better partner in the present.

Sometimes, Evelyn would feel like they weren't making any progress. But she had to remind herself that every small step was a step in the right direction. She celebrated their victories, no matter how small they were, and focused on the positive changes they had made.

Patience wasn't always easy, but Evelyn knew it was essential to their marriage's survival. She had to trust the process, trust Adam, and most importantly, trust herself. She was committed to being patient, even if it meant taking two steps forward and one step back.

In the end, Evelyn's patience paid off. She and Adam had built a stronger and more fulfilling marriage than they ever thought possible. They had learned that patience, understanding, and commitment were the keys to a successful relationship.

Twenty-Two

The Trust

Trust was a major issue for Evelyn and Adam after the affair. But over time, they learned to trust each other again. They started to rebuild the trust brick by brick, through consistent communication and actions.

***

Evelyn and Adam both knew that trust was essential to their relationship. They knew that without trust, their marriage would be built on a weak foundation. So, they made a conscious effort to rebuild the trust between them.

At first, it was difficult. Evelyn would often question Adam's actions and motives. She would second-guess everything he did, wondering if he was being truthful. Adam, on the other hand, felt like he was walking on eggshells around Evelyn. He was afraid to say or do anything that might set her off.

But slowly, they started to make progress. They began to communicate more openly and honestly with each other. They shared their feelings, their fears, and their hopes for the future.

As they talked, they started to understand each other's perspectives better. They learned how to listen to each other without judgment or defensiveness. And they started to see that they were both committed to making their marriage work.

One day, during a conversation, Evelyn expressed her concerns to Adam. "I know it's going to take time for me to fully trust you again," she said, "but I don't want to keep second-guessing your every move. Can you help me feel more secure in our relationship?"

Adam nodded, understanding her worries. "Of course," he replied. "I'll do whatever it takes to show you that I'm committed to us. And I promise to be patient and understanding as you work through your trust issues."

Over time, their efforts to communicate more openly and honestly with each other extended beyond just checking in throughout the day. They also made a conscious effort to have deeper conversations about their thoughts and feelings, even when it was uncomfortable.

One evening, while they were sitting outside on the porch, Evelyn broached a topic that had been weighing on her mind. "Adam, I've been feeling really anxious lately," she said. "I don't know why, but I just can't shake this feeling."

Adam listened attentively, his eyes locked on hers. "I'm sorry to hear that, Evelyn. Is there anything I can do to help?"

Evelyn took a deep breath. "Honestly, I just need you to be here for me. To listen and support me, even if you don't understand why I'm feeling this way."

Adam nodded. "Of course, Evelyn. I'm here for you, always. And if you ever need to talk, I'm here to listen."

Their conversation was uncomfortable at first, but it opened the door to a deeper level of trust and understanding between them. By being vulnerable and honest with each other, they were able to strengthen their bond and support each other in ways they never thought possible.

As they continued to communicate openly and honestly with each other, they also found that their disagreements were becoming less frequent and less intense. They were able to find common ground more easily and resolve conflicts with more grace and understanding.

Their efforts to improve their communication and deepen their connection had paid off in ways they never could have imagined. They were happier, more fulfilled, and more in love than ever before.

As the weeks turned into months, Evelyn and Adam started to rebuild the trust between them. They made promises to each other and worked hard to keep them. They were patient with each other, knowing that rebuilding trust takes time.

They also started to take actions that demonstrated their commitment to each other. Adam would often surprise Evelyn with small gestures of kindness, like bringing her breakfast in bed or leaving her little notes around the house. Evelyn, in turn, would make an effort to show Adam that she trusted him.

For example, she would let him go out with his friends without worrying about what he was doing or who he was with. She would also share her own feelings more openly with him, letting him see that she trusted him to listen and respond with kindness.

Through these consistent communication and actions, Evelyn and Adam started to rebuild the trust that had been broken. They still had moments of doubt and insecurity, but they were able to work through them together.

They also started to see the positive effects that trust had on their relationship. They were more relaxed around each other, and they had a deeper connection than they had before. They felt like they were truly partners, working together to build a life they both wanted.

Of course, there were still challenges along the way. There were moments when old fears and insecurities would resurface, and they would have to work through them all over again. But each time they did, they became stronger as a couple.

Through it all, Evelyn and Adam learned that trust is not something that can be given or received easily. It is something that must be earned over time, through consistent communication and actions. And they were willing to do whatever it takes to rebuild the trust in their relationship.

As they looked back on their journey, they felt proud of how far they had come. They knew that they still had work to do, but they were confident that they could face any challenge together. They had rebuilt the trust between them, brick by brick, and they knew that their love was stronger for it.

They started to rebuild the trust brick by brick, through consistent communication and actions.

Twenty-Three

The Appreciation

Evelyn and Adam learned to appreciate each other in new ways. They started to show gratitude for the little things and to recognize the effort each other was putting into their relationship.

* * *

Their newfound appreciation for each other was reflected not only in their actions but also in their conversations. Adam would often express his gratitude towards Evelyn and tell her how much he valued her patience and understanding, and how much he admired her strength and resilience.

"I don't know how I would have made it through some of the tough times without you," Adam said one day while they were driving back from a family outing. "You've been my rock."

Evelyn smiled and reached for his hand. *"I'm just happy to be here for you,"* she replied. "I love you."

"I love you too," Adam said, squeezing her hand.

Evelyn also made an effort to thank Adam for his dedication and commitment to making their marriage work.

"You always put in so much effort to make sure we're happy and taken care of," she said one evening as they sat on the porch, watching the sunset. *"I appreciate you more than you know."*

Adam grinned. *"I do it because I love you,"* he said. *"And because I know that we're stronger together than we are apart."*

As their love and appreciation for each other continued to grow, they also surprised each other with small acts of kindness. Adam would bring home Evelyn's favorite snack or plan a surprise outing for the two of them, while Evelyn would leave little love notes for Adam to find throughout the day.

Their marriage wasn't perfect, but it was filled with moments like these - moments of love, gratitude, and kindness that made all the struggles worth it.

Through these gestures, Evelyn and Adam were able to build a deeper level of trust and intimacy in their relationship. They had both learned that it was the little things that mattered the most and that showing appreciation and gratitude could go a long way in keeping their love strong.

This newfound appreciation helped to strengthen their bond and create a deeper sense of connection. They realized that they were no longer taking each other for granted, and that every little act of kindness and affection had the power to make a significant impact on their relationship.

Their newfound appreciation for each other's qualities and strengths also led to deeper conversations and a greater understanding of each other. One evening, while they were enjoying a quiet dinner at home, Evelyn asked Adam what he admired most about her.

"I admire your kindness," Adam said without hesitation. *"You always see the best in people, even when they don't deserve it. And you have a way of making me feel loved and appreciated that no one else does."*

Evelyn blushed and smiled. *"Thank you, Adam,"* she said. *"What about you? What do you think I should appreciate more about you?"*

Adam thought for a moment before answering. *"I think you should appreciate my sense of humor more,"* he said. *"I know it doesn't always* come across the right way, but I love making you laugh. And I think it's important to have humor in our relationship, especially when things get tough."

Evelyn nodded, realizing that she had taken Adam's sense of humor for granted in the past. *"You're right,"* she said. *"I do appreciate your humor, even if I don't always show it. I'm glad you make me laugh."*

As they continued to appreciate each other's unique qualities and strengths, they also found that they were able to handle difficult situations more effectively. They no longer saw each other as obstacles or adversaries, but as partners who could work together to overcome any challenge, their relationship continued to grow and flourish. They felt more connected and supported than ever before, and they knew that their love was stronger than any obstacle that they might face.

It was through this newfound appreciation that Evelyn and Adam realized that they had truly overcome the affair and were on the path to a happy and healthy future together.

Twenty-Four

The Forgiveness

Forgiveness was a crucial part of the healing process for Evelyn and Adam. They had to forgive each other for the pain they had caused and the mistakes they had made.

* * *

Over the next few weeks, Evelyn and Adam had several conversations about forgiveness. They talked about the pain they had caused each other and the effort it would take to move past it.

One evening, Evelyn brought up the topic again. *"I've been thinking a lot about forgiveness, Adam. And I've realized that it's not just about you. I have to forgive myself too. I've been carrying so much guilt and shame about not standing up for myself, about not being a better wife."*

Adam put his arm around her. *"Evelyn, you don't have anything to feel guilty about. You've been an amazing wife, and you've done nothing wrong. I'm the one who made a mistake, and I'm the one who needs to ask for forgiveness."*

Evelyn leaned into him, feeling comforted by his words. *"Thank you, Adam. I needed to hear that. But I still have a long way to go before I can fully forgive you."*

"I know," Adam said. "But I'm here for you, every step of the way. And I will do whatever it takes to make things right between us."

As the weeks went on, Evelyn and Adam continued to work on forgiveness. They attended therapy sessions, read books, and had many conversations about the topic. And slowly but surely, they started to make progress.

One day, while they were out on a walk together, Adam stopped Evelyn and took her hand. "I know I've said it before, but I want to say it again. I am so sorry for what I did. And I will spend the rest of my life making it up to you."

Evelyn looked up at him, her eyes filled with tears. "I know, Adam. And I appreciate all the effort you've put in. But I'm still struggling to forgive you completely."

Adam nodded, understanding. "I know it's a process, Evelyn. And I will be patient with you. But I promise you, I will never stop trying to earn your forgiveness."

Over time, Evelyn started to feel more at peace with what had happened. She was still hurt, but she was also starting to see the progress they had made. And she realized that forgiveness was not just about letting go of the past, but also about building a stronger future together.

.

Twenty-Five

The Self-Care

Evelyn realized that she needed to take care of herself in order to be a good partner. She started to prioritize self-care and made time for the things that made her happy and fulfilled.

* * *

Evelyn had been feeling exhausted lately. Between her work, therapy sessions, and trying to rebuild her marriage, she didn't have much time for herself. One day, she decided to take a day off and do things that made her happy.

Adam noticed her excitement as she talked about her plans for the day. *"You seem really happy about this,"* he said.

"I am," Evelyn replied. *"I realized that I need to take care of myself if I want to be a good partner to you. And today, I'm going to do things that bring me joy."*

Adam smiled. *"That's great. What do you have planned?"*

"Well, I'm going to start with a yoga class this morning. Then, I'm going to get a massage and have lunch at my favorite café. After that, I might go see a movie or just spend some time reading in the park," Evelyn explained.

"That sounds wonderful," Adam said. *"I'm glad you're making time for yourself."*

Evelyn nodded. *"It's important for both of us. I can't give my best to our marriage if I'm not taking care of myself."*

Adam paused for a moment before speaking. *"You're right. I should do the same."*

Evelyn looked at him, surprised. *"What do you mean?"*

"I mean, I should take care of myself too," Adam said. *"I've been so focused on repairing our relationship that I haven't taken much time for myself either."*

Evelyn smiled. *"That's a great idea. What would you like to do?"*

Adam thought for a moment. *"Well, I've been wanting to try a new hiking trail that's not too far from here. Maybe I'll do that this weekend."*

Evelyn nodded. *"That sounds like a great way to unwind and recharge."*

As the day went on, Evelyn felt more and more relaxed. She enjoyed her yoga class, savored her lunch, and even treated herself to a slice of cake for dessert. By the time she got home, she felt refreshed and ready to tackle the rest of the week.

"Hey, how was your day?" Adam asked as she walked through the door.

Evelyn grinned. *"It was amazing. I feel so much better now."*

"I'm glad," Adam said. *"I'm going to start planning my own day of self-care soon."*

Evelyn smiled. *"I think that's a great idea. We both deserve to take care of ourselves."*

Over the next few weeks, Evelyn and Adam continued to prioritize self-care. They made time for activities that made them happy and fulfilled, whether it was going for a hike, trying a new restaurant, or simply taking a relaxing bath. They found that when they took care of themselves, they were better able to show up as partners to each other.

As they reflected on their progress, Evelyn realized that self-care was an important part of their marriage. *"We should make a pact to always prioritize our own well-being,"* she said to Adam one night.

Adam nodded. *"I agree. We can't be good partners if we're not taking care of ourselves first."*

Evelyn smiled. *"Exactly. So, let's promise to always make time for the things that make us happy and fulfilled."*

"I promise," Adam said.

"Me too," Evelyn replied. *"I think this is one of the keys to a happy marriage."*

Twenty-Six

The Intimacy

Intimacy was something that had suffered in their marriage after the affair. But as they continued to work on their relationship, Evelyn and Adam started to rediscover their physical and emotional connection.

* * *

Evelyn and Adam had been working hard to rebuild their relationship. They had made progress in communicating better, understanding each other's needs, and rebuilding trust. But there was one area of their marriage that still needed improvement - intimacy.

Evelyn felt hesitant to be intimate with Adam after the affair. She didn't know if she could trust him again, and she worried that he might hurt her again. But as they continued to work on their relationship, Evelyn started to feel more comfortable with the idea of being intimate with Adam.

One night, as they lay in bed together, Evelyn turned to Adam and said, *"I've been thinking a lot about us and our intimacy. I want to work on it, but I'm still scared. How can we make this work?"*

Adam took her hand and said, *"I understand that you're scared, and I don't want to rush you. We can take things slow and do what feels right for both of us. I want to make you feel safe and loved."*

Evelyn smiled at Adam's words and leaned in for a kiss. As they kissed, Evelyn felt a rush of emotions - fear, excitement, and love. She knew that this was going to be a journey, but she was willing to take it with Adam.

Over the next few weeks, Evelyn and Adam started to explore their intimacy. They took things slow, focusing on touching and being close without the pressure of sex. They cuddled more, held hands, and hugged.

One night, as they lay in bed together, Adam whispered in Evelyn's ear, *"I love you. I want to show you how much I love you."*

Evelyn looked at him and smiled. She knew that he meant it, and she was ready to take the next step. They made love that night, and it was different than before. It was more emotional, more intimate, and more loving.

Afterwards, as they lay in bed together, Adam said, *"I'm so glad we're doing this together. I love you so much, Evelyn."*

Evelyn smiled and said, *"I love you too, Adam. I'm so grateful for this second chance."*

As they continued to work on their intimacy, Evelyn and Adam started to feel closer than ever before. They made time for each other, prioritized their relationship, and communicated openly about their needs and desires.

One night, as they were getting ready for bed, Evelyn turned to Adam and said, *"I feel so close to you right now. I never thought we could get here after everything that happened."*

Adam smiled and said, *"I know. It's been a journey, but I'm glad we're here. I feel so connected to you."*

Evelyn kissed Adam and said, *"I'm so grateful for you, Adam. Thank you for never giving up on us."*

Adam pulled her close and said, *"I'll never give up on us, Evelyn. I love you too much."*

As they drifted off to sleep, Evelyn and Adam knew that they still had work to do, but they were confident that they could overcome any obstacle together.

Twenty-Seven

The Communication

Communication was key in rebuilding their marriage. Evelyn and Adam started to have honest and vulnerable conversations with each other, sharing their fears, hopes, and dreams.

In one of their therapy sessions, Evelyn expressed her fear of Adam straying again. *"I know we've made a lot of progress, but sometimes I still worry that you might cheat on me again,"* she said, her voice trembling.

Adam reached over and took her hand. *"I understand why you would feel that way, and I'm sorry for the pain I've caused you. But I want you to know that I'm committed to our marriage, and I will do everything in my power to make sure nothing like that ever happens again."*

Evelyn smiled weakly, appreciating his words but still feeling anxious. *"I know you're trying, and I believe you. But I think I need some reassurance, too. Maybe we could have a weekly check-in where we talk about how we're feeling and what we need from each other."*

Adam nodded. *"That's a good idea. I want to do everything I can to make you feel safe and secure in our marriage."*

Over the next few weeks, they started to implement their weekly check-ins. They would set aside time each Sunday to talk about their feelings, any concerns they had, and how they could support each other. It was a small but important step in improving their communication.

As they continued to practice open communication, Adam and Evelyn also started to be more affectionate with each other. One day, as Adam was cooking dinner, he walked over to Evelyn and wrapped his arms around her from behind.

Evelyn smiled and leaned into his embrace. *"What's this for?"* she asked.

"Just because," Adam replied, planting a soft kiss on her cheek. *"I love you."*

Evelyn turned around and hugged him tight. *"I love you too,"* she said.

From then on, they made a conscious effort to show affection to each other every day. Adam would surprise Evelyn with a hug or a kiss on the cheek, and she would reciprocate by cuddling up to him on the couch while they watched TV.

During one such evening, as they were watching their favorite show, Evelyn turned to Adam and said, *"I'm so grateful for you."*

Adam looked at her and smiled. *"Why's that?"*

"Because you make me feel loved and appreciated every day," Evelyn replied. *"And I hope I do the same for you."*

"You do," Adam said, taking her hand in his. *"I feel so lucky to have you in my life."*

Evelyn leaned in and kissed him softly. *"I feel the same way,"* she said.

As they continued to grow in their affection for each other, they also grew in their love and commitment. Their marriage wasn't perfect, but it was real and filled with moments of joy, love, and connection. And that was all they could ever ask for.

One night, after a particularly emotional therapy session, they ended up lying in bed together, talking and holding each other. Adam traced circles on Evelyn's back, and she let out a contented sigh.

"I feel like we're really making progress," she said, looking up at him.

"I do, too," he replied, smiling down at her. *"I'm so grateful that we're in this together."*

Evelyn nodded, feeling grateful as well. *"Me too. And I'm glad we're finally learning how to communicate better. It feels like we're finally getting back to the way things used to be."*

They spent the rest of the night talking and laughing, feeling closer than they had in a long time. As they drifted off to sleep, Evelyn knew that they still had work to do, but she was grateful for how far they had come.

Twenty-Eight

The Growth

Evelyn and Adam's relationship continued to grow and evolve. They learned to adapt to each other's changing needs and to support each other through the ups and downs of life.

* * *

As time went on, Evelyn and Adam's relationship continued to grow and evolve. They both recognized the importance of being there for each other, not just during the tough times, but also during the good times. They made a conscious effort to show each other appreciation and love on a daily basis.

"I just want you to know how much I appreciate you," Adam said one night as they sat on the couch together. "You've been through so much with me, and yet you still stick by my side."

Evelyn smiled and leaned her head on his shoulder. "I appreciate you too," she replied. "You've put in so much effort to make things right between us. It hasn't been easy, but I can see how much you've grown and changed."

Adam took her hand and gave it a gentle squeeze. "I have to thank you for that. You never gave up on me, even when I didn't deserve it."

Evelyn shook her head. *"I wasn't perfect either. We both made mistakes, but we've grown from them."*

They continued to talk, sharing their hopes and dreams for the future. It was a far cry from the days when they would avoid any sort of conversation that might lead to conflict.

As their relationship continued to grow, they learned to adapt to each other's changing needs. When Evelyn started a new job that required her to work longer hours, Adam stepped up and took on more responsibilities around the house.

"I know you're tired when you get home, so I wanted to make dinner tonight," he said one evening as she walked through the door.

Evelyn smiled gratefully. *"Thank you. You really didn't have to do that."*

Adam shrugged. *"I wanted to. I know you've been working hard, and I appreciate everything you do for us."*

Their communication also continued to improve. They had learned to have honest and vulnerable conversations with each other, even when it was uncomfortable.

"I know I messed up in the past, but I want you to know that I'm committed to making this work," Adam said one night as they lay in bed together.

Evelyn turned to face him. *"I know you are. And I believe you. But we have to keep talking about our feelings and what's going on between us. We can't sweep things under the rug."*

Adam nodded in agreement. *"I'm willing to do whatever it takes to keep our relationship strong."*

As they continued to support each other through the ups and downs of life, their relationship grew stronger than ever before. They had learned that with patience, commitment, and communication, anything was possible.

Twenty-Nine

The Milestones

As they approached major milestones in their marriage, like their fifth wedding anniversary, Evelyn and Adam reflected on how far they had come and how much they had grown as a couple.

* * *

Evelyn and Adam sat together on their living room couch, flipping through their wedding album as their fifth anniversary approached.
"Can you believe it's already been five years?" Evelyn said, looking up at Adam with a smile.
"It feels like a lifetime, in a good way," Adam replied, placing a hand on her knee.
Evelyn nodded, "Yeah, we've been through so much together."
Adam leaned in to kiss her cheek, "And we've come out stronger on the other side."
Evelyn smiled, "Definitely. But there were times when I wasn't sure we'd make it to this milestone."
"I know," Adam said, "But we did. And I'm grateful for that."
Evelyn took a deep breath, "Me too. But it hasn't always been easy."

Adam looked at her with concern, "What do you mean?"

Evelyn hesitated for a moment before speaking, "*Sometimes I worry that we've worked so hard on rebuilding our marriage that we've lost some of the spontaneity and fun we used to have.*"

Adam nodded, "*I see what you mean. But we can work on that, too. We don't have to sacrifice one for the other.*"

Evelyn smiled, "*I know. I just don't want us to forget why we fell in love in the first place.*"

Adam squeezed her hand, "*We won't. We'll keep working on our relationship and finding new ways to grow and connect.*"

As their anniversary approached, Evelyn and Adam continued to reflect on their marriage and the progress they had made. They talked about their future goals and dreams, and made plans to celebrate their love and commitment to each other.

On the day of their anniversary, Evelyn woke up to find a bouquet of flowers and a love note from Adam on her bedside table. She felt a surge of gratitude and love for her husband, and knew that they had come so far since their darkest days.

At dinner that night, as they clinked their glasses together, Adam smiled at Evelyn and said, "*Here's to us. To five years of marriage, and to many more to come.*"

Evelyn's heart swelled with love and gratitude. She knew that their marriage wasn't perfect, but it was real and honest and filled with moments like this - moments of joy and connection that made all the struggles worth it.

"To us," she echoed, smiling back at Adam.

They spent the rest of the evening talking and laughing, feeling grateful for the life they had built together. As they cleared the plates and put the kids to bed, they held hands and whispered words of love and affection to each other.

"I love you, Evelyn," Adam said as they settled into bed.

"I love you too, Adam," she replied, snuggling into his embrace.

As they drifted off to sleep, Evelyn felt a sense of contentment wash over her. She knew that their marriage wasn't always going to be easy, but as long as they had each other, they could face anything together. And that was a feeling worth toasting to.

As they hugged each other tightly before bed, Evelyn whispered, *"I love you, Adam."*

Adam held her close, *"I love you, too, Evelyn. Happy anniversary."*

Evelyn smiled, feeling grateful for their journey and for the love that had kept them together.

Thirty

The Reflections

Evelyn and Adam continued to reflect on their past and how it had shaped their relationship. They acknowledged the mistakes they had made but chose to focus on the progress they had made.

* * *

As they sat together on the couch, Evelyn turned to Adam and said, "Do you ever think about how far we've come?"

Adam nodded, "All the time. It's hard to believe it's been almost two years since everything happened."

Evelyn took a deep breath, "Sometimes, I still can't believe we made it through all of that. But I'm so grateful that we did."

Adam took her hand, "Me too. We've both grown so much since then. I'm proud of us."

Evelyn smiled, "Me too. I think we've learned a lot about ourselves and each other."

Adam nodded, "Definitely. And I think we've learned to communicate better too. Remember when we used to avoid difficult conversations?"

Evelyn laughed, *"How could I forget? But now, I feel like we can talk about anything."*

Adam leaned in, *"I love that about us. We can be open and honest, even when it's hard."*

Evelyn squeezed his hand, *"It's what makes our relationship stronger."*

They sat in comfortable silence for a moment before Evelyn spoke up again, *"Do you ever regret staying with me after everything?"*

Adam shook his head, *"No, I don't. I know we've been through a lot, but I believe that our love is worth fighting for."*

Evelyn felt a wave of emotion wash over her, *"I feel the same way. I know we're not perfect, but I believe in us."*

Adam smiled, *"Me too. And I'm excited to see what the future holds for us."*

Evelyn leaned into him, feeling grateful for their love and the progress they had made together.

Thirty-One

The Gratitude

Gratitude became a daily practice for Evelyn and Adam. They made a point to express their appreciation for each other and to celebrate the good in their lives.

* * *

In the morning, Evelyn woke up to the smell of coffee and bacon coming from the kitchen. She smiled as she got out of bed and made her way to the kitchen where Adam was cooking breakfast.

"*Good morning, beautiful,*" Adam said, greeting her with a kiss on the cheek.

"*Good morning, handsome,*" Evelyn replied, returning the kiss.

As they sat down to eat breakfast, Adam spoke up. "*I just wanted to say how grateful I am for you. You make my life so much better.*"

Evelyn smiled. "*I'm grateful for you too. I don't know where I'd be without you.*"

Later that day, as they were driving to the grocery store, Evelyn turned to Adam. "*I just wanted to thank you for being so supportive of me lately. You always know how to make me feel better.*"

Adam smiled. *"Of course, Evelyn. We're in this together, through thick and thin."*

Evelyn nodded. *"I know. And I'm so grateful for that."*

As they were checking out at the grocery store, Adam took Evelyn's hand and gave it a squeeze. "I'm grateful for our life together, Evelyn. I wouldn't want it any other way."

Evelyn squeezed his hand back. *"Me neither, Adam. I'm grateful for every moment we've had together."*

As they walked out of the store and back to their car, Evelyn couldn't help but feel overwhelmed with gratitude for Adam and their life together. She knew that they had been through a lot, but she was grateful for the journey that had brought them to where they were now.

Thirty-Two

The Goals

Evelyn and Adam started to set goals for their future together. They talked about their dreams and aspirations and made plans to work towards them as a team.

* * *

Evelyn sat across from Adam at the kitchen table, sipping her coffee. "I've been thinking a lot about our future lately," she said, setting down her mug.

Adam looked up from his newspaper. "Me too," he replied. "What's on your mind?"

"Well, I was thinking about how we haven't really set any goals for ourselves as a couple," Evelyn said. "I think it's important that we have something to work towards together."

Adam nodded in agreement. "I've been thinking the same thing," he said. "Do you have any ideas?"

Evelyn took a deep breath. "I'd like us to start saving up for a down payment on a house," she said. "It doesn't have to be anything fancy, just a place that we can call our own."

Adam smiled. *"I like that idea,"* he said. *"I think it's important that we have a place where we can put down roots and start a family."*

Evelyn felt a flutter of excitement in her stomach. *"You want to have kids?"* she asked.

Adam nodded. *"Someday, yeah,"* he said. *"I know we've got a lot of work to do on our relationship first, but I think we could make really great parents."*

Evelyn's heart swelled with love for her husband. *"I think so too,"* she said, reaching across the table to take his hand.

As the weeks went by, Evelyn and Adam continued to talk about their goals and aspirations. They decided that they wanted to take a trip to Europe, to visit the places they had always dreamed of seeing. They also talked about starting a business together, using their combined skills and talents to build something of their own.

"I've been doing some research on starting a catering business," Adam said one evening as they cooked dinner together. *"I think it could be really lucrative, and we could both use our culinary skills."*

Evelyn smiled. *"That sounds like a great idea,"* she said. *"I've been wanting to do something more creative with my marketing background. We could make a really great team."*

Adam nodded. *"I agree,"* he said. *"We'll have to start doing some serious planning and research, but I think we could make it work."*

As the months passed, Evelyn and Adam continued to work towards their goals. They started saving for a down payment on a house and researching the real estate market. They also began planning their trip to Europe, deciding which cities they wanted to visit and what sights they wanted to see.

"It's going to be so amazing," Evelyn said one night as they looked at pictures of Paris. *"I can't believe we're actually going to do this."*

Adam wrapped his arm around her. *"I know,"* he said. *"I can't wait to experience all of these things with you."*

As they sat there, planning their future together, Evelyn and Adam felt more in love than ever before. They knew that there would be challenges ahead, but they were confident that they could face them together, as a team.

Thirty-Three

The Support

As they worked towards their goals, Evelyn and Adam found support in each other. They were each other's biggest cheerleaders and knew that they could count on each other no matter what.

* * *

In the early morning, Evelyn woke up feeling anxious about an important job interview she had that day. She tried to calm herself down but couldn't shake off the nerves. She turned to Adam, who was still sleeping, and gently shook him.

"Eve, what's wrong?" Adam asked, rubbing his eyes.

"I can't stop thinking about my interview today," Evelyn replied, her voice trembling.

Adam sat up and put his arm around her. "You're going to do great, Evelyn. I believe in you."

Evelyn leaned into him, feeling his warmth and support. "Thank you, Adam. I don't know what I'd do without you."

"You don't have to worry about that," Adam said, kissing the top of her head. "I'll always be here for you."

Later that day, after Evelyn's interview, she called Adam with the good news. *"I got the job!"* she exclaimed.

"That's amazing, Evelyn!" Adam replied. *"I'm so proud of you."*

"Thank you, Adam," Evelyn said, tears of joy streaming down her face. *"I couldn't have done it without you."*

Adam and Evelyn continued to support each other through their individual pursuits. When Adam decided to go back to school to pursue a new career, Evelyn encouraged and supported him every step of the way.

"I don't know if I can do this," Adam said, feeling overwhelmed with his studies.

"Yes, you can," Evelyn said firmly. *"You're smart and capable, and I believe in you."*

Adam smiled, feeling grateful for Evelyn's unwavering support. *"Thank you, Evelyn. You always know how to make me feel better."*

As they pursued their individual goals, Adam and Evelyn also made plans for their future together. They talked about buying a house, starting a family, and traveling the world.

"I want us to see the world together," Evelyn said, looking dreamily into Adam's eyes.

"Me too," Adam said, taking her hand. *"I can't wait to see what our future holds, Evelyn."*

As they fell asleep that night, Adam and Evelyn felt grateful for the support they had in each other and excited for the future they were building together.

Thirty-Four

The Challenges

There were still challenges along the way, but Evelyn and Adam faced them together. They knew that they were stronger together than they were apart.

* * *

In the midst of their journey, Evelyn and Adam encountered various challenges that tested their commitment to each other. They faced financial struggles when Adam lost his job and had difficulty finding another one. It was a stressful time for the couple, but Evelyn assured Adam that they would get through it together.

Another challenge came when Evelyn's father fell ill and had to be hospitalized. She was devastated and felt overwhelmed, but Adam was there for her every step of the way. He took care of her father while she worked and made sure that Evelyn was taking care of herself.

Their communication was put to the test when they disagreed on how to discipline their children. Evelyn believed in a more lenient approach, while Adam was more strict. After a heated argument, they eventually came to a compromise and agreed to be consistent in their discipline.

Evelyn also struggled with self-doubt and feelings of insecurity, especially when she compared herself to Adam's ex-lover. Adam reassured her that he loved her for who she was and that their past mistakes did not define their present or future.

Another challenge came when they realized that they had grown apart in some areas of their lives. Evelyn wanted to pursue her passion for photography, while Adam was content with his job as a salesman. They worked together to find a balance and support each other's dreams.

Despite these challenges, Evelyn and Adam remained committed to each other and their marriage. They continued to prioritize communication and understanding, even when it was difficult. They knew that their love for each other was worth fighting for.

"Sometimes it feels like we're going through a never-ending storm," Evelyn said one night as they sat on the couch together. *"But as long as we're in this together, I know we can weather anything."*

Adam nodded in agreement. *"I wouldn't want to face any of this with anyone else but you,"* he said, taking her hand in his. *"We're a team, and we'll always have each other's backs."*

Evelyn smiled, feeling grateful for the love and support of her husband. She knew that no matter what challenges came their way, they would face them together, as partners and as best friends.

Thirty-Five

The Reflection

Evelyn continued to reflect on her own growth and the changes she had made in her life. She realized that she was a stronger, more resilient person because of what she had gone through.

* * *

Evelyn sat quietly on the couch, lost in thought. Adam noticed her distant expression and asked, *"What's on your mind?"*

"I was just thinking about how much I've changed over the past few years," Evelyn replied.

Adam nodded in agreement. *"You have changed a lot, for the better. I'm proud of you."*

"I'm proud of myself too," Evelyn said, a small smile forming on her lips. *"I never thought I could be this strong."*

"You're one of the strongest people I know," Adam said, placing a comforting hand on her shoulder.

Evelyn leaned into his touch, feeling grateful for his support. *"I wouldn't have been able to do it without you,"* she said softly.

Adam smiled. *"We've been through a lot together. It's made us both stronger."*

Evelyn took a deep breath. *"Sometimes I still have moments of doubt, though. Like, what if something happens and we can't handle it?"*

"We'll handle it," Adam said firmly. *"We've proven that we can overcome anything if we work together."*

Evelyn nodded, feeling reassured. *"I know you're right. It's just hard to shake off that fear sometimes."*

Adam squeezed her shoulder gently. *"I understand. But we can't let fear hold us back. We've come too far to let that happen."*

"You're right," Evelyn said, taking another deep breath. *"I just need to keep reminding myself of that."*

"We'll remind each other," Adam said with a smile.

Evelyn smiled back, feeling grateful for his unwavering support. Together, they would continue to reflect on their journey and grow stronger every day.

Thirty-Six

The Renewed Vows

As a symbol of their commitment to each other, Evelyn and Adam decided to renew their vows. They gathered their closest friends and family and recommitted themselves to their marriage.

* * *

Evelyn and Adam had come a long way since the affair that had threatened their marriage. As they approached their tenth wedding anniversary, they wanted to do something special to commemorate the occasion. Evelyn suggested renewing their vows, and Adam immediately loved the idea.

"*It's a beautiful way to show our commitment to each other,*" he said, taking Evelyn's hand.

Evelyn smiled, feeling a warm glow in her chest. "*I was thinking we could do it at the beach, just the two of us,*" she said.

Adam's eyes lit up. "*That's perfect. We can exchange vows and then take a walk on the beach.*"

As they planned their ceremony, they decided to invite their closest friends and family members to share the day with them. Evelyn's sister offered to officiate the ceremony, and Adam's best friend agreed to be his best man.

As the day of the ceremony approached, Evelyn and Adam were both excited and nervous. They had been through so much together, and this vow renewal was a chance to celebrate their journey.

As Evelyn walked down the aisle towards Adam, she felt a rush of emotions. Seeing him standing there, looking at her with so much love, made her heart swell with gratitude.

"You look beautiful," Adam whispered as they met at the altar.

Evelyn smiled and squeezed his hand. *"You don't look too bad yourself,"* she teased.

As they exchanged vows, Evelyn felt tears spring to her eyes. They had been through so much, but their love had only grown stronger.

"I promise to love and cherish you for all the days of my life," Adam said, looking deeply into Evelyn's eyes.

"And I promise to do the same," Evelyn said, her voice breaking with emotion.

As they kissed, the sun broke through the clouds, casting a warm glow over the beach. Evelyn and Adam were both overcome with a sense of peace and joy.

As they walked along the beach after the ceremony, hand in hand, Evelyn and Adam felt a renewed sense of commitment to each other. They knew that they had come a long way, but there was still so much ahead of them.

"I love you," Adam said, breaking the comfortable silence between them.

"I love you too," Evelyn replied, smiling up at him.

They continued walking, their feet sinking into the soft sand, the ocean waves crashing against the shore. In that moment, they knew that they had everything they needed – each other.

Thirty-Seven

The Trust Issues

Even after rebuilding their trust, there were moments when Evelyn would feel insecure or doubt Adam's loyalty. But she learned to communicate her feelings and work through them with Adam's support.

* * *

In the early days of their renewed commitment, Evelyn struggled with trusting Adam again. She found herself questioning his every move, wondering if he was being truthful with her.

Adam noticed Evelyn's apprehension and wanted to reassure her. *"Evelyn, I understand that you're still trying to trust me again, and I respect that. But I want you to know that I am committed to you and our marriage. I will do whatever it takes to earn your trust back,"* he said.

Evelyn nodded, feeling slightly reassured. *"I know, Adam. It's just hard sometimes. But I'm willing to work on it with you."*

As time passed, Evelyn's trust in Adam slowly started to rebuild. But there were still moments when she felt insecure, especially when Adam was away from home for long periods of time.

"Evelyn, I understand why you're worried. But I want you to know that I will never betray your trust again. I love you and I will always be honest with you," Adam said, trying to reassure her.

Evelyn took a deep breath, trying to calm her anxiety. *"I know you love me, Adam. And I do trust you, but it's hard not to let my mind wander sometimes,"* she replied.

Adam reached out and took her hand. *"I understand. But remember, we're in this together. We can work through anything as long as we communicate and trust each other,"* he said.

Evelyn nodded, feeling grateful for Adam's support. She knew that rebuilding trust took time, but she was willing to put in the effort.

As time went on, Evelyn's trust in Adam continued to grow. She found herself worrying less and less about his loyalty and focusing more on building a happy and healthy marriage together.

"I never thought I would be able to trust you again, Adam. But I'm so grateful that we were able to work through this together," Evelyn said one day.

Adam smiled and took her hand. *"I'm grateful too, Evelyn. We've come so far and I'm excited to see where our future takes us,"* he replied.

Evelyn leaned in and kissed Adam, feeling happy and content in their renewed love and trust for each other.

Thirty-Eight

The Openness

Evelyn and Adam continued to be open with each other, even when it was uncomfortable or difficult. They knew that honesty was the foundation of their relationship.

* * *

Evelyn and Adam sat on the couch, their faces serious as they discussed a sensitive topic.

"I know it's hard to talk about, but I need you to be open with me," Evelyn said, taking Adam's hand.

Adam nodded. "*I understand. I promise to be honest with you, no matter what.*"

This commitment to openness had become a cornerstone of their relationship, and they knew it was necessary to maintain their trust and connection. Over time, they had learned to have difficult conversations and share their deepest fears and insecurities.

For example, when Evelyn had expressed her concerns about Adam's work colleague, he had listened patiently and reassured her of his loyalty. They had worked through her insecurities together, and it had only strengthened their bond.

In another instance, Adam had opened up about his own struggles with anxiety and how it had affected his behavior in the past. Evelyn had listened with empathy and reassured him that she was there for him no matter what.

Their openness had also led to positive changes in their relationship. They had started to express their desires and needs more clearly, which had led to a more fulfilling and satisfying intimate life.

"I really like it when you do that," Evelyn said with a smile after Adam had tried something new in bed.

"I'm glad you enjoyed it. I just want to make you happy," Adam replied, his eyes full of love.

Their commitment to openness had not only strengthened their relationship but also improved their individual well-being. They were able to express themselves freely without fear of judgment or rejection.

"I'm proud of you for speaking up at work today," Adam said one evening. *"I know it wasn't easy, but it shows how much you've grown in your confidence."*

Evelyn smiled, feeling a sense of pride and validation. *"Thank you for noticing. It means a lot."*

Their conversations were not always easy, but they knew that the benefits far outweighed the discomfort. Their openness had allowed them to truly know and understand each other, which had led to a deeper level of intimacy and connection.

"I have to tell you something," Evelyn said one night, her voice shaking slightly. *"I'm scared about the future."*

Adam took her hand and squeezed it gently. *"I'm scared too. But we'll face it together. Whatever happens, we'll be okay as long as we have each other."*

Evelyn felt a sense of comfort wash over her at his words. Their openness had allowed them to share their fears and find strength in each other.

"I just want to thank you for always being there for me," Evelyn said one day, looking at Adam with gratitude in her eyes.

Adam smiled. *"Of course, that's what partners are for. I'm here for you, always."*

Their commitment to openness had allowed them to build a strong foundation of trust and love. They knew that they could rely on each other no matter what life threw their way.

Thirty-Nine

The Anniversary

On their fifth wedding anniversary, Evelyn and Adam celebrated how far they had come. They reminisced about their journey and looked forward to what was to come.

* * *

Evelyn and Adam woke up on their fifth wedding anniversary feeling grateful and blessed. They had come a long way since the affair and were excited to celebrate their love and commitment to each other.

"I can't believe it's been five years already," Evelyn said, snuggling closer to Adam. "It feels like just yesterday we were walking down the aisle."

"I know, time flies when you're having fun," Adam replied, kissing her forehead. "But it also feels like we've been through so much together."

Evelyn nodded, tears welling up in her eyes. "I'm just so grateful for you, Adam. You've stuck by me through thick and thin, and I couldn't have done it without you."

"You don't have to thank me, Evelyn. I love you, and I always will," Adam said, pulling her into a tight embrace.

As they got ready for the day, Evelyn and Adam exchanged heartfelt gifts. Adam had written Evelyn a love letter and bought her a beautiful necklace, while Evelyn had framed their wedding vows and put together a scrapbook of their memories together.

"*I can't believe you remembered that I've been eyeing this necklace for months!*" Evelyn exclaimed, tears of joy in her eyes.

Adam smiled, taking the necklace from her and clasping it around her neck. "*Of course I remembered, I pay attention to the little things.*"

After getting ready, they decided to spend the day doing things they loved. They started by going on a hike in the mountains, enjoying the fresh air and beautiful scenery.

"*I feel so alive when we're out here,*" Adam said, taking Evelyn's hand in his. "*It's like the world fades away, and it's just you and me.*"

Evelyn smiled, feeling the same way. "*I know what you mean, Adam. It's moments like these that remind me how much I love being with you.*"

After the hike, they headed to a spa for a couple's massage and some pampering. As they relaxed, they talked about their hopes and dreams for the future.

"*I can't wait to see what the next five years hold for us,*" Evelyn said, closing her eyes and sinking deeper into the massage table.

"*I know, it's exciting to think about all the possibilities,*" Adam replied, his own eyes closed.

After the massage, they got dressed up for a fancy dinner at their favorite restaurant. They toasted to their love and commitment to each other and enjoyed a delicious meal.

As they finished dessert, Adam reached into his pocket and pulled out a small box. Evelyn's heart raced as he got down on one knee.

"*Evelyn, these past five years have been the best of my life. I love you more than anything in this world, and I want to spend the rest of my life making you happy. Will you marry me again?*"

Evelyn gasped, tears streaming down her face. "*Yes, yes, of course I will!*"

Adam slipped a new ring onto her finger, and they embraced, kissing passionately. The restaurant erupted in applause and cheers.

"I love you so much, Evelyn," Adam whispered, holding her close.

"I love you too, Adam," Evelyn replied, feeling overwhelmed with joy and gratitude.

As they left the restaurant hand in hand, Evelyn and Adam knew that they had come so far in their journey together, and they were excited for what the future held.

Forty

The Reflection

Evelyn reflected on the progress they had made and how much stronger their relationship was because of it. She realized that love is not just a feeling but a choice that you make every day.

* * *

As Evelyn sat in her favorite spot on the couch, she looked over at Adam and smiled. *"Can you believe how far we've come?"* she asked.

Adam turned to her, a look of contentment on his face. *"It's amazing, isn't it? I never thought we could get back to this place."*

Evelyn nodded. *"It wasn't easy, but it was worth it. I feel like we're so much stronger now than we ever were before."*

Adam took her hand in his. *"I agree. I'm so grateful that we were able to work through our issues and come out the other side."*

Evelyn leaned her head on his shoulder. *"Me too. And I think it's important to keep reflecting on our journey and how far we've come. It helps us appreciate what we have now."*

Adam nodded. *"I couldn't agree more. And it's a good reminder that we're not invincible. We have to keep working on our relationship every day."*

Evelyn looked up at him, a small smile playing on her lips. "I'm glad you said that. Because there's something I wanted to talk to you about."

Adam furrowed his brow in concern. "What is it?"

Evelyn took a deep breath. "I know we've come a long way, but sometimes I still feel insecure. Like maybe you'll cheat again or that you don't really love me."

Adam's expression softened. "Oh, Evelyn. I'm sorry you feel that way. I want you to know that I love you more than anything in this world. And I would never do anything to hurt you like that again."

Evelyn felt a weight lift off her shoulders. "Thank you, Adam. I know it's irrational, but sometimes those thoughts just creep in."

Adam squeezed her hand. "I understand. And I promise to always be honest and open with you. That's the only way we can continue to build trust."

Evelyn smiled gratefully at him. "You're right. And speaking of trust, I wanted to let you know that I have a work conference coming up in a few weeks. And there will be a few social events that I'm expected to attend."

Adam looked at her curiously. "Okay. Is there something you're worried about?"

Evelyn hesitated for a moment. "Well, there will be some colleagues there who I used to flirt with before we worked on our marriage. And I just wanted to be upfront with you about it, in case it made you uncomfortable."

Adam smiled reassuringly. "Thank you for telling me. But I trust you, Evelyn. And I know you would never do anything to jeopardize our relationship."

Evelyn felt a surge of gratitude for Adam's trust in her. "Thank you, Adam. That means a lot to me."

As their conversation wound down, they sat in comfortable silence, each lost in their own thoughts. But Evelyn couldn't help but feel a sense of contentment wash over her. She was grateful for the progress they had made and the open communication they shared. And she knew that as long as they continued to work on their relationship, they could overcome any obstacle that came their way.

Forty-One

The Empathy

Evelyn and Adam learned to empathize with each other's struggles and support each other through difficult times. They became each other's safe haven.

* * *

Evelyn and Adam had both been through their fair share of challenges, both together and individually. But as they continued to work on their relationship, they started to develop a deeper sense of empathy for each other.

As Adam continued to share his feelings with Evelyn, he felt a sense of relief wash over him. He hadn't realized how much he had been bottling up his emotions until he had the opportunity to talk to someone who genuinely cared about him.

Evelyn knew that Adam had a tendency to keep his feelings to himself, and she was grateful that he had opened up to her. She knew how important it was for him to feel heard and understood, especially during times of stress and anxiety.

After Adam finished talking, Evelyn suggested that they take a walk around the neighborhood to clear their minds and get some fresh air. They held hands and walked in silence for a few moments, enjoying the warmth of the sun on their faces.

As they walked, Evelyn spoke up. "You know, Adam, I really appreciate it when you share your feelings with me. It helps me understand what you're going through and how I can support you."

Adam smiled, feeling a sense of gratitude for his wife. "I know I can always count on you to be there for me," he said.

Evelyn squeezed his hand. "Of course, Adam. We're a team, and we'll get through anything together."

As they continued their walk, Adam felt a sense of peace wash over him. He knew that he had a partner who would always be there for him, no matter what. And that was the greatest comfort of all.

Another time, Evelyn felt grateful for Adam's understanding and support. She had been feeling overwhelmed and unappreciated at work, and his words of encouragement helped to lift her spirits.

"Thank you, Adam," she said, giving him a grateful smile. "I really needed to hear that."

Adam hugged her tightly, feeling a sense of protectiveness over his wife. "I'm here for you, Evelyn. Always."

Evelyn leaned into his embrace, feeling a sense of comfort in his arms. She knew that no matter how tough things got, she had someone in her corner who would always be there for her.

As they sat on the couch together, Adam suggested that they order in some takeout and watch a movie. Evelyn nodded, feeling grateful for the simple pleasures of life and the love and support of her husband.

As they settled in to watch the movie, Evelyn felt her spirits lifting. She knew that the road ahead wouldn't always be easy, but she also knew that with Adam by her side, she could face anything that came their way.

Together, they enjoyed a night of relaxation and comfort, reminded once again of the power of love and support in the face of adversity.

As they continued to practice empathy with each other, they also started to become more aware of each other's needs. Adam noticed that

Evelyn tended to get anxious in social situations, so he made a point to be more attentive and supportive when they attended events together. Evelyn noticed that Adam was feeling overwhelmed with work, so she took on more household responsibilities to help ease his stress.

Through their conversations, Evelyn and Adam also learned to validate each other's emotions. They acknowledged that it was okay to feel angry, sad, or frustrated, and that it was important to express those feelings in a healthy way. They supported each other through difficult emotions and offered comfort and validation when needed.

They also practiced active listening, taking the time to fully understand each other's perspectives before responding. They asked questions and sought clarification when needed, rather than jumping to conclusions or making assumptions.

Their empathy extended beyond just their relationship with each other. They also learned to empathize with others outside of their relationship, such as family members and friends. They offered support and understanding when others were going through difficult times, and showed compassion and kindness in their interactions with others.

Through their empathy and understanding, Evelyn and Adam's relationship became even stronger. They became each other's safe haven, a place where they could be vulnerable and honest without fear of judgment. They knew that no matter what challenges they faced, they would always have each other's support and understanding.

Forty-Two

The Growth Mindset

Evelyn and Adam adopted a growth mindset, recognizing that there is always room for improvement and that they could continue to grow together.

* * *

Evelyn and Adam sat down at the kitchen table, a fresh pot of coffee steaming between them. They had been talking about the future and how they wanted to continue to grow as individuals and as a couple.

Adam took a sip of his coffee before speaking. *"I've been reading this book about the growth mindset, and it's really got me thinking. We've come so far, but there's still so much we can do to keep growing together."*

Evelyn nodded, intrigued. *"Tell me more."*

"Well," Adam said, *"I think it's about embracing challenges and seeing them as opportunities for growth, rather than just obstacles to overcome. And also, being open to learning and trying new things."*

Evelyn smiled, feeling inspired. *"I like that. I think it's easy to get comfortable and stop pushing ourselves. But if we have a growth mindset, we can keep challenging ourselves to be better."*

They spent the rest of the morning talking about different ways they could adopt a growth mindset in their daily lives. They talked about trying new hobbies, taking on new challenges at work, and exploring new ways to communicate and connect with each other.

As they continued to embrace a growth mindset, they noticed positive changes in their relationship. They were more open to feedback and willing to learn from each other's perspectives. They also found that they were more resilient in the face of challenges, knowing that they could overcome them together.

One example of their growth mindset in action was when Adam decided to take up running. He had never been much of a runner before, but he was curious about the physical and mental benefits of the sport.

Evelyn was supportive and encouraged him to pursue it, even though it meant adjusting their schedules and finding new ways to spend time together. As Adam trained for his first 5K, they went on runs together and talked about their goals and challenges.

When Adam finally completed the race, Evelyn was there cheering him on, feeling proud of how far they had come together.

Another example was when Evelyn decided to go back to school to pursue a new career. It was a big step for her, and she had to juggle work, school, and their relationship.

But Adam was there every step of the way, offering encouragement and support. He even helped her study for exams and proofread her papers.

As Evelyn completed her degree and landed her dream job, they both felt a sense of accomplishment and pride in how they had grown together.

Through their growth mindset, Evelyn and Adam continued to push themselves and each other to be the best versions of themselves. They learned that there is always room for improvement and that their relationship could continue to evolve and thrive.

Forty-Three

The Resilience

Through the ups and downs of their relationship, Evelyn and Adam became more resilient. They knew that they could overcome anything together.

* * *

Evelyn and Adam had been through a lot in their relationship, but they had learned to bounce back from tough situations. They knew that they had to be resilient if they wanted to make their marriage work in the long run.

"*I'm so proud of us,*" Evelyn said to Adam one day. "*We've been through so much, but we've come out the other side stronger.*"

Adam smiled and took her hand. "*I couldn't agree more,*" he said. "*We've learned to weather the storms and come out even closer on the other side.*"

They had faced many challenges together, from infidelity to financial struggles to health issues. But each time, they had leaned on each other for support and come out even stronger.

"*I think our resilience comes from our ability to communicate,*" Evelyn said. "We're not afraid to have those tough conversations and work through our problems together."

Adam nodded. "And we never give up on each other," he said. "We know that we're in this for the long haul and that we have to keep pushing through the tough times."

They also recognized the importance of self-care in building their resilience. They made time for the things that made them happy and fulfilled, like exercise, hobbies, and time with friends and family.

"Taking care of ourselves is just as important as taking care of each other," Adam said. "If we're not at our best, then our relationship won't be either."

Evelyn agreed. "And we have to be willing to ask for help when we need it," she said. "We can't do everything on our own, and it's okay to lean on others for support."

They also celebrated their successes and milestones along the way. They recognized that even small victories were worth celebrating, and that helped them stay motivated and positive.

"I think our resilience also comes from our mindset," Evelyn said. "We try to focus on the positives and learn from our mistakes instead of dwelling on them."

Adam smiled. "And we always make sure to find ways to have fun and enjoy each other's company," he said. "That keeps us connected and happy."

They knew that there would be more challenges ahead, but they were confident that they could handle them together. Their resilience was a testament to the strength of their love and commitment to each other.

Forty-Four

The Gratefulness

Evelyn and Adam continued to express their gratitude for each other and the life they had built together. They realized that their love had been tested and had come out stronger.

* * *

In the quiet moments of their life together, Evelyn and Adam often found themselves reflecting on how far they had come. They would sit on the couch with cups of tea in hand, gazing out the window and talking about the good things in their lives.

"I'm grateful for you," Evelyn said, taking Adam's hand in hers. "*I don't know where I would be without you.*"

Adam smiled, his eyes crinkling at the corners. "*I'm grateful for you too, Evelyn. You've made me a better person.*"

As they continued to talk, their conversation turned to their relationship and how it had changed over the years.

"Do you remember when we first got together?" Adam asked. "We were so young and naïve."

Evelyn chuckled. "Yes, but we were in love. That's all that mattered."

Adam nodded. *"But we've come so far since then. We've been through so much, and yet we're still here."*

Evelyn squeezed his hand. *"I think it's because we've always been grateful for what we have. Even when things were tough, we never forgot how lucky we were to have each other."*

Adam leaned in and kissed her softly. *"I'm grateful for this moment right now. Just you and me."*

As they pulled away from each other, they both felt a renewed sense of gratitude for each other and the life they had built together. They knew that it wasn't always easy, but it was always worth it.

Later that week, as they were getting ready for bed, Adam turned to Evelyn and said, *"I've been thinking about something. I want to plan a special trip for us. A second honeymoon."*

Evelyn's eyes widened in surprise. *"Really? That sounds amazing."*

Adam nodded. *"I want to do something special for our ten-year anniversary. It's coming up soon, and I want it to be memorable."*

Evelyn grinned. *"I can't wait. It's going to be wonderful."*

In the weeks leading up to their anniversary, they made plans and prepared for their trip. They talked excitedly about all the things they wanted to do and see.

On the day of their departure, as they sat on the plane, holding hands, Evelyn felt a sense of gratefulness wash over her. She looked at Adam and felt a wave of love and appreciation for him.

"Thank you for this," she said, leaning over to kiss him.

Adam smiled. *"Anything for you, my love."*

As they embarked on their second honeymoon, they knew that it would be a time for reflection, growth, and gratitude. They were excited to explore new places and make new memories together.

Forty-Five

The Forever After

Evelyn and Adam's love story was not perfect, but it was real. They had fought for their marriage and their love and had come out on the other side stronger and more committed than ever. They knew that their forever after was worth fighting for.

* * *

As Evelyn and Adam sat together on their porch, watching the sunset, they reflected on their journey. "Can you believe how far we've come?" Evelyn asked.

Adam turned to her, his eyes filled with love. "It's been a wild ride, but I wouldn't have wanted to go through it with anyone else."

Evelyn smiled, feeling grateful for the man sitting beside her. "I'm just happy we made it through. We fought hard for our forever after."

Adam nodded. "And we're not done fighting. We'll keep choosing each other every day."

Evelyn leaned her head on his shoulder. "I'm so grateful for you, Adam. You're my rock."

Adam wrapped his arm around her, pulling her closer. *"I'm grateful for you too, Evelyn. You've made me a better man."*

As they sat in comfortable silence, they both knew that their love was stronger than ever. They had faced their demons and come out on the other side.

But they also knew that their journey was not over. There would be more challenges, more obstacles to overcome. And they were ready to face them together.

The next morning, as they sipped their coffee, Evelyn brought up a new topic. *"I've been thinking about our families lately."*

Adam looked up from his paper. *"What about them?"*

"Well, we've been so focused on rebuilding our relationship that we haven't had much time to deal with the extended family drama."

Adam nodded in agreement. *"That's true. I think we've been avoiding it because it's just so exhausting."*

Evelyn sighed. *"I know, but it's not going to go away on its own. We need to figure out how to handle it."*

Adam put down his paper, giving her his full attention. *"You're right. What do you suggest?"*

"I think we need to have a family meeting. Sit down with everyone and lay out our expectations. Let them know that we're a team and that we won't tolerate any negativity or drama."

Adam smiled, feeling proud of his wife. *"I think that's a great idea. Let's make it happen."*

As they continued to talk and plan, Evelyn and Adam knew that their forever after would not always be easy. But they were committed to facing it together, with love and respect for each other and a determination to overcome any obstacle.

And as they closed the chapter on their past struggles and looked forward to their future, they knew that their journey was far from over. But they were ready for whatever lay ahead.

Conclusion

In conclusion, "Rebuilding Love" by David Olubiyi is a powerful and inspiring story of love, forgiveness, and resilience. Through the ups and downs of their relationship, Evelyn and Adam show us that love is not perfect, but it's worth fighting for.

The book emphasizes the importance of communication, empathy, and self-reflection in any relationship. It shows us that we can overcome even the most challenging obstacles if we are willing to work hard and commit to each other.

Ultimately, "Rebuilding Love" is a reminder that no matter how far we have drifted apart or how broken our relationship may seem, it's never too late to start rebuilding. With patience, understanding, and a willingness to grow together, anything is possible.

This book is a must-read for anyone who has ever struggled in a relationship and is looking for hope and inspiration. It is a story that will touch your heart and leave you feeling inspired to pursue the kind of love that lasts a lifetime.

Acknowledgement

I would like to express my gratitude to everyone who helped bring this book to life.

Firstly, I would like to thank my family for their unwavering support and encouragement throughout this journey. Your love and belief in me kept me going, even during the toughest moments.

I also want to extend my deepest appreciation to my editor and publishing team for their guidance, expertise, and patience. Your valuable feedback and suggestions have greatly contributed to the success of this book.

To my friends and colleagues who have provided their encouragement and support, I am grateful. Your kind words and gestures have been a source of motivation for me.

Finally, to the readers who have chosen to pick up this book, I hope it brings value and insights that will positively impact your relationships. Your interest and support mean the world to me.

Thank you all for being a part of this journey.

www.ingramcontent.com/pod-product-compliance
Lightning Source LLC
Chambersburg PA
CBHW041455010526
44107CB00014B/1049